# THE
# POLITICS
# OF
# MANAGEMENT
# CONSULTING

# THE
# POLITICS
# OF
# MANAGEMENT
# CONSULTING
## by Gerald L. Moore

PRAEGER

PRAEGER SPECIAL STUDIES • PRAEGER SCIENTIFIC

New York • Philadelphia • Eastbourne, UK
Toronto • Hong Kong • Tokyo • Sydney

**Library of Congress Cataloging in Publication Data**

Moore, Gerald L.
　The politics of management consulting.

　Bibliography: p.
　Includes index.
　1. Business consultants. I. Title.
HD69.C6M58 1984　　　658.4'6　　　83-19231
ISBN 0-03-069249-0 (alk. paper)

Published in 1984 by Praeger Publishers
CBS Educational and Professional Publishing
a Division of CBS Inc.
521 Fifth Avenue, New York, NY 10175 USA

© 1984 by Praeger Publishers.

456789 052 987654321

Printed in the United States of America
on acid-free paper

This book is dedicated posthumously to
Frances Louise

# Acknowledgments

I am indebted to Bogdan Denitch and to Dean Savage for their constructive theoretical suggestions as well as for their critical readings of the various drafts of the manuscript.

I am grateful to Edgar Borgatta for his direction and resourcefulness in the initial preparation of the manuscript.

I am also grateful to Irving Gregory for his personal criticism and influence that has not only led to the publication of this manuscript, but given direction to my professional career as well.

Many others were helpful in different ways. I want to acknowledge Marlene, Miriam, Morton, Bob, and Jack.

I am deeply indebted to Joseph Bensman for making this all possible by first inspiring me several years ago to undertake a project of this nature, and for his endless series of questions and refinements. Most of all I would like to thank him for his insight, dedication and obvious expertise.

Of course, a very special thanks and appreciation to Julia for her overall assistance and her multiple contributions to this book.

# Contents

## PART III
## CONCLUSION

# PART I
# Introduction

# O N E

# Overview

## GENERAL STATEMENT

To grow or maintain their existence, organizations must respond to change rationally and effectively. These changes may emanate from external or internal environmental causes as well as from individual or group pressures.

Change may be sought by the organization for a number of reasons. One reason for seeking change is to **increase the productivity** of the organization. Productivity may be viewed not only as organizational output, such as the company product or service, but as unit cohesiveness and drive in the forms of morale or pride of workers. Units can be considered in terms of sections, departments, or divisions within the company. A similar reason for instituting change is to **alter dysfunctional behavior** that is preventing the achievement of organizational goals. This dysfunction is largely exhibited in terms of conflict between the personal goals of employees and organizational goals.

Change may also be sought for the purpose of **enhancing the organization's image**, both inside and outside the company. Most organizations wish to be considered "modern" companies who keep up with new technologies and trends. Thus new methods or ideas may be implemented for the purpose of doing something "new"—whether or not it has other benefits for the organization.

Another pressure creating the need for change comes from *recognition of new social norms*: the need to do things differently or to satisfy new laws. Two examples are Occupational Safety and Health Administration (OSHA) regulations and Equal Employment Opportunity (EEO) laws enacted by the federal government, both of which have had far-reaching effects on many companies.

Other reasons for change stem from internal pressures: the attempt *to pacify dissidents* within the company or *to solidify or expand one group's power* in the company. In these cases change is sought by those in the organization who would benefit from their improved political position in the company—not necessarily for the benefit of the organization itself.

Still another reason for implementing change in the organization arises when old goals and objectives that have not been successful need supplanting. After a period of time, *unsuccessful goals* must be replaced or the organization cannot maintain itself. In a similar fashion change provides a mechanism for *adopting new goals* once others have been achieved, thereby allowing the organization to grow.

As social structures become more complex, business has turned to outside and specialized internal experts to help them cope with the clamor for more decision making at lower managerial levels. Two factors have stimulated the use of management consultants, who have proliferated, to provide solutions to various problems caused by the stresses and strains that have emerged in the corporate apparatus: (1) the request for changes in older, bureaucratic models to allow for more decentralized decision making and the delegation of authority with responsibility at lower levels of management and (2) increased social legislation.

This study will focus on the intended and unintended effects of the intervention of management consultants on the corporations who are their clients. It is hypothesized that while management consulting firms are brought in for a number of specific purposes by specific company executives to solve specific problems as perceived by those executives, they may or may not "solve" the specific presenting problems for which they are retained and in doing so may aggravate other problems in the organization or produce new ones. In some cases the problems they create may be more serious than those they were employed to solve.

The question will be raised as to whether the consultant should bring other than the presenting problem to the attention of the client even though the firm's doing so may be viewed as a means of creating additional demand for its services or as a power play to extend its influence in the company.

To test the main hypothesis, a case study detailing one company's use of five management consultants will be presented. All of the data have been gathered in the course of the author's experience as an executive and management consultant. The case study will examine managerial consulting assignments from the (reconstructed) initial assignment, to the analysis of the presenting problem, to the presentation of findings and recommendations, to the consequences of all these for the corporation.

The attempt will be made to establish whether the consulting firm has had specific positive benefits for the company in question, or no impact, or unintended consequences that are either positive or negative. The determination of positive or negative impacts will be stated in terms of their consequences for the organization as a functioning totality and not for individual members or units within it.

## BACKGROUND ON MANAGEMENT CONSULTING

Management consulting as a professional service and as a method of implementing change is not confined to any particular type of organization. It operates in all areas of organizations, public and private, and in all aspects of their operations: technological, managerial, financial, personnel, and public relations. In North America there are about 3,500 management consulting firms, and the use of management consultants has become common practice.

Management consulting had its origin in free market economies where independent companies used consultants in many different ways. Over the years consulting has spread into government as well as private business. Most consulting assignments, however, have traditionally been confined to industrial and commercial enterprises. From these sectors consulting has expanded to transport, catering, banking, and insurance. Important management consulting has been carried out for trade unions, sports and religious organizations, and international governmental organizations.

Management consulting grew out of the *scientific management movement* of the early 1900s. **Frederick Taylor**, considered the father of scientific management, began as an engineer in the steel industry. In 1911 he formulated principles to increase productivity. He stressed the need for cooperation between workers and managers to increase the surplus produced. To apply his principles, there was an increase in the use of time and motion techniques. Taylor retired at the age of 45 and became a consultant to industry.

Followers of Taylor also branched out and became independent consultants in the steel industry and others. **Carl Barth** and **Henry Gantt** were management engineering consultants in the steel industry. **Frank and Lillian Gilbreth** applied their ideas with Taylor's and became consultants on the improvement of human productivity. Lillian Gilbreth was one of the United States's first industrial psychologists and combined the interest in efficiency with an interest in the human aspects of the workers. She believed that worker dissatisfaction was generated by management's lack of interest in the workers as people.

The work in scientific management stimulated a simultaneous development of industrial psychology and sociology applied to industry. This led to the growth of sociological approaches to human relations and management.

**Hugo Munsterberg**, working out of Harvard University around 1900, began applying the behavioral sciences to the scientific management theories. He combined the principles of engineering efficiency with an emphasis on the psychological qualities of workers. He believed that this approach was necessary for analyzing each task in terms of the mental qualities required and then selecting workers capable of performing them.

For that purpose he developed vocational tests to screen out unfit job applicants. Some of the psychological factors he studied were attention, fatigue, monotony, and social influences on work output.

**Elton Mayo**, who was on the faculty of the Wharton School of Finance at the University of Pennsylvania and later taught at the Harvard Business School, was also a management consultant for industry. Mayo, **Fritz Roethlisberger**, and **William Dickson**—along with other Harvard researchers—undertook a series of experiments at the *Hawthorne plant* of Western Electric between 1927 and 1932.[1] Before Mayo stepped in, the National Research Council had made a study of the effects of illumination and other conditions on workers and their productivity (from 1924 to 1927). By 1927 the researchers concluded that lighting was only a minor influence on the employees' output. Whether they raised or lowered illumination, productivity increased. They felt that attempts to measure experimental effects were unsuccessful because it was difficult to control the many factors that interacted in affecting productivity. Western Electric wanted to continue the experiments; thus in 1927 they called on Mayo and his associates.

Mayo tried to isolate the effects on output by introducing other changes in the environment: smaller groups, rest periods, and a more sociable climate. Output increased whether or not the changes were introduced and again when they were eliminated. To try to determine the reason for the increase in productivity, extensive interviews were conducted with 20,000 employees about their attitudes. From these interviews the effects of peer pressure on performance stood out. To study this further, the researchers selected a group of employees working on the same job. In this case the output was restricted and production did not rise. This was attributed to worker peer pressure.

Two major conclusions were drawn from these studies. One was that the novelty or attention generated by the study and the researchers themselves affected employees' attitudes favorably, and this led to increased productivity. This is called the *Hawthorne effect*. The second result was that the type of supervision and climate also affected output. If the supervisor paid attention to the workers and allowed a free exchange of communication, production rose. In the situation where the supervisor was not interested in understanding group behavior, workers restricted output.

Although the Hawthorne studies were not definitive in their findings, they launched the human relations approach in management and sparked further research.

**Chester Barnard**, an executive for the Bell Telephone Company, wrote *The Functions of the Executive*[2] in 1938, based on his own observations of the activities of managers. He emphasized the importance of communication between manager and worker to establish a cooperative system where the worker puts forth maximum effort on the job. This was one of the major influences altering the concept of the manager's job to include more than the authority to direct or lead workers. Barnard believed that the manager must elicit the worker's consent and cooperation to do the job well. Barnard's writings stimulated interest in motivation, decision making, leadership styles, and organizational relationships.

By the 1940s the contributions and involvement of the social scientists in consulting and management theory were expanding into several areas. Much of the application of social science theory to management was an outgrowth of the psychological testing developed to test soldiers during World War I and the tight labor market during World War II. This development of personality, intelligence, and interest inventory tests was used to screen job applicants for industry.

After World War II, consulting in marketing and in various newer management techniques, such as operations research and systems design, was expanded. This was followed by changes in the concepts of consulting in general management to embrace prospective problems of business strategy, long-range planning, decision making, and organization development.

At the same time the increasing prestige and utility of the physical sciences in industry reinforced the growing managerial faith in the application of the social sciences to industry. The chemical, electrical equipment, and aircraft industries were those most committed to research in the physical sciences. They established research labs and commissioned research that could be applied to their own industry. These same industries became interested in social science research and its application to industry. Social scientists from universities such as Harvard continued to be sought after as consultants to business. Large universities—such as Harvard University, the University of Michigan, Ohio State University, and the University of Pennsylvania—conducted research in business organizations. This gave the professors credibility in the business world, and they were hired as consultants to apply their knowledge gained through research. Social scientists from these schools, such as **Rensis Likert**, **Edwin Fleishman**, and **Frederick Herzberg**, became well-known consultants to business.

According to **Philip Shay**, management consultants have played an active role in supplementing the work of managers in industry. The founders of the managing consultant profession were responsible for establishing management as a separate discipline of study and research:

> The development of almost every accepted technique—work measurement, compensation and incentive plans, improved work methods, systems analysis, market research, information systems, budgetary control and the like—has been the joint work of consultants and men in industry. And they have also made distinct contributions to such central problems of managing a business as the design of the business, corporate strategy, human organization, manager development, the management of relations, innovation and keeping the enterprise relevant to the economic and social environment in which it functions.[3]

After World War II the *human relations approach* to industrial problems expanded as a trend in industry. This was an interdisciplinary field borrowing from both psychology and sociology. Out of this background came an emphasis on motivation and small groups, leadership, and communications. The human relations philosophy asserted that the business organization is a social system and that employees are motivated by the human relationships within the system.

The human relations school believed that employee participation was needed to provide employees with job satisfaction and improve morale. The assumption was that a satisfied and happy employee was a more productive worker. Thus motivation was provided not only by monetary incentives—as the scientific management approach believed—but by personal needs to be liked and to belong in a group as well. To improve morale and satisfy these needs, managers should keep employees informed and allow them to participate in decision making, so the theory went. The way the manager treated subordinates was seen as crucial to good morale and, thereby, productivity.

Using the relatively new techniques of *role playing* and *sociometry* developed by **Jacob Moreno**, the human relations field grew as more and more managers believed that human relations was the key to getting employees to work harder. Moreno, a psychiatrist, was concerned with the impact of group life on its individual members. His technique of diagramming preferences among workers in a group, that is, **sociograms**, provided a means of studying the relationships among group members.

Although by the 1950s the assumption that a happy worker was a productive worker was shown not to be true by such researchers as Likert, Herzberg, **Abraham Zaleznik**, and others, many of the influences of the human relations school have remained.[4]

Despite the growing acceptance of human relations in industry, a number of companies were skeptical: they awaited evidence in terms of productivity gains. The use of excessive jargon served to alienate some segments of industry, with some managers labeling the industrial social scientist as "impractical, ignorant and possibly crazy. With time, however, even executives joined in the sport and used the jargon themselves. . . . As the human relations approach gained steam, fewer and fewer managers had the necessary conviction or will to resist the fad."[5]

One of the key concepts of the human relations approach was *motivation*. Though the scientific management approach had assumed that money was the greatest incentive for workers, some social scientists now proposed that workers needed other, less tangible rewards. *Herzberg's motivation-hygiene theory*, based on *Maslow's need hierarchy*, was the catalyst for this idea. Herzberg proposed that unless people were given the opportunity to satisfy the intangible needs, such as personal growth and advancement, there would be no real motivation. This idea appealed to management because it did not require increasing salaries or pay. Other social scientists such as **John**

**Atkinson** and **Victor Vroom** opposed this trend by claiming that monetary rewards were, indeed, important and that individual needs, personalities, and expectations of employees must be taken into account in determining motivation.

Regardless of the lack of agreement on a common theoretical basis for an acceptable theory of motivation, everyone agreed that motivation was an important key for management. Maslow's theory of need hierarchy gained increasing acceptance along with Herzberg's adaptation of that concept for use in the work situation as a tool that managers could utilize to stimulate motivation.

Researchers on group dynamics theories defined such attributes and concepts in their own terms as *cohesiveness, sociometry, conformity, power and influence*, and *leadership behavior* and applied them to studies of work groups in industry.[6] **Leadership**, long considered important in management, began to be the focus of new approaches. Among some managers improving styles of leadership and gaining the respect of workers became an objective replacing the assertion of power and authority. Starting from Barnard's emphasis on cooperation, more social scientists stressed the importance of the relationship between the leader of the work group (the manager) and the group members (subordinates).[7]

At first the research on leadership styles concentrated on trying to identify **traits** that would distinguish the "leaders."[8] When it was seen that no particular traits were exhibited only by leaders and not by followers,[9] efforts then turned to identifying what **behavior** made a leader effective in a particular situation.

One of the most widely used models using a **situational approach** to leadership styles was that of **Robert Tannenbaum** and **Warren Schmidt**.[10] They described leadership styles in terms of a continuum of authority used by the leader and the area of freedom allowed to group members (see Table 1-1). In this human relations approach managerial theorists tried to move away from the traditional use of the "autocratic" style, where the manager plays the dominant role in making decisions, toward the use of the "democratic" style, where there is a sharing and communication with subordinates. The human relations advo-

**TABLE 1-1**
**LEADERSHIP STYLES CONTINUUM**

| Autocratic | Democratic | Group Centered |
|---|---|---|
| | | |

The Leader's Authority

Areas of Freedom for Group Members

| Autocratic | Democratic | Group Centered |
|---|---|---|
| Leader decides and tells group | Leader asks members but leader decides | Leader and group members decide together (share authority) | Leader defines limits and lets group decide | Members decide —leader is a member of group |

*SOURCE:* Reprinted by permission of the *Harvard Business Review.* A figure from "How to Choose a Leadership Pattern" by Robert Tannenbaum and Warren H. Schmidt (May/June 1973). Copyright © 1973 by the President and Fellows of Harvard College; all rights reserved.

cates believed that democratic leadership would produce more work. The possibility that this type of leadership might result in at least some benefits was enough to stimulate companies to sponsor leadership training programs to include management with the advocated style. Training was targeted primarily at first-line supervisors, who were believed to have the most direct impact on workers' productivity.

By the 1950s industrial programs in human relations were common, using techniques based on sociology, psychology, and the Harvard case study method to teach managers "people skills" as well as other management skills. One such program conducted at International Harvester Company was studied by researchers at Ohio State University. It was typical of the training given to thousands of first-line supervisors.[11]

The Harvester program included 5,000 supervisors enrolled in a course devoted to personal development (21 hours of speaking, writing, planning, and logical thinking), human relations (29 hours of human behavior, industrial relations, industrial organization and control, and application of human relations), and company operations and finance (17 hours). In the program the democratic leadership pattern was taught as the most desirable leadership style for supervisors to use.[12]

According to Baritz, the new approach became a fad in industry, without any actual research demonstrating that such training accomplished its promised results. "As usual, a few social scientists dissented, questioning the human-relations training being given to foremen and its effectiveness.... Despite such doubts, industry went on its determined way of finding out whether or not more highly trained foremen could in fact increase output, morale and loyalty while reducing costs, grievances and conflict."[13] Whether or not leadership training could produce the desired effects remained very much a question.

Much of the research that was conducted on leadership effectiveness was done in universities. There were two main research centers that were established to conduct studies in business on leadership effectiveness: the Bureau of Business Research at Ohio State University and the Institute for Social Research at the University of Michigan.

In the 1950s Fleishman identified two independent dimensions by factor analysis of data from leader behavior questionnaires at Ohio State University. These major dimensions, as defined by Fleishman, were:

> *Initiating structure* (S): Acts which imply that the leader organizes and defines the relationships in the group, tends to establish well defined patterns and channels of communication and ways of getting the job done (e.g., he assigns people to particular tasks, he emphasizes deadlines, etc.).

> *Consideration* (C): Behavior indicating . . . mutual trust, respect, a certain warmth and rapport between the supervisor and his group . . . the tolerance for two-way communications seemed to become a key feature of this dimension. High scores on items such as "he makes those feel at ease when talking to them," "He puts suggestions into operation,". . . . A low score would indicate the supervisor who is arbitrary and impersonal in his relations.[14]

He found these dimensions consistently important in assessing industrial supervisors over a wide range of studies using two questionnaires that measure the amount of structure and consideration as perceived by the supervisor and his subordinates. The **Leadership Opinion Questionnaire (LOQ)** is a Likert-type attitude scale that assesses how the supervisor thinks he should behave in his leadership role. The **Leader Behavior Description Questionnaire (LBDQ)** measures subordinate perceptions of supervisory behavior. Although it initially was thought that there was one "best" pattern of consideration and structure scores for effective leaders, later research showed that this was not the case. In a review of C and S research, **Abraham Korman** states that there is a great deal of inconsistency in the results of studies relating leader patterns of C and S to effective performance and "there is very little evidence that leadership behavioral and/or attitudinal variation," as defined by scores on the LOQ or LBDQ, "are predictive of later effectiveness and/or satisfaction criteria."[15]

Other research, conducted by **Fred Fiedler**, led to the theory that situational factors (**position power, task structure**, and **leader-member relations**) interact with certain personality attributes in determining leadership effectiveness. Fiedler found that a reliable leader-personality variable can be obtained through a **_Least Preferred Coworker (LPC) score_**.[16] "It is obtained by asking an individual to think of all the people with whom he has ever worked, and to describe the one person in his life with whom he found it most difficult to work on a common task . . . by marking a set of 16 to 20 items on an eight-point, bipolar scale of the semantic differential type."[17] Examples of items on the scale are pleasant-unpleasant, accepting-rejecting, helpful-frustrating. The LPC score is the sum of the item scores, with the positive pole of each item giving a high score. A high LPC score is interpreted as reflecting a motivation to relate to others. A low score is interpreted as reflecting a motivation for task accomplishment.[18] The LPC is a motivational or personality variable that Fiedler himself says is difficult to interpret but that is independent of other personality or attitude scales and has been found to be reliable in extensive studies on leadership. The LPC is the one variable that has been consistently related to performance.[19]

The majority of the research has supported Fiedler's hypothesis that low-LPC leaders perform better in very favorable situations and in unfavorable situations, while high-LPC leaders tend to perform better in conditions of intermediate favorableness.[20]

Many consultants have used these leadership effectiveness theories to develop and sell their own leadership training programs to clients. These have become quite popular even though research has not established that these training programs are effective. So far there has been little examination of the research on the effectiveness of leadership or management training programs. Although voluminous literature has been written (between 1945 and 1949 there were an average of 55 studies per year; between 1950 and 1953, there were an average of 152 per year;[21] in 1974, however, a survey of leadership theory and research found it necessary to analyze over 3,000 books and articles in the field),[22] very little has been written about the methodological evaluation of leadership/management training. The dearth of evaluation studies is largely attributable to the complexity and difficulty in establishing controlled conditions and the inability to isolate variables in the real world as opposed to the laboratory.

Another reason is that scientifically controlled evaluations usually involve extensive follow-up, which may mean extra time away from the job for participants. Time lost from the job can be quite costly and, in addition to the high cost of the study itself, makes evaluation too inconvenient and expensive. Still another reason for the lack of evaluation in corporations is the difficulty in tracking participants over a period of time to see if the training was effective. With the rapid changes occurring in most companies, many managers do not remain on the same job, retain the same superior, or even stay in the same department.

Even when evaluation is done, it is difficult to attribute positive effects to the training. There are other factors that contribute to visible effects such as the relationship between the trainer and participant or the additional attention being given to managers as a result of their participation in the evaluation study.

In 1967 Fiedler complained about the lack of studies of the effects of leadership training:

> Organizations have been more than happy to spend money on training programs but they have been considerably less eager to find out whether the training really does any good. Moreover, personnel research has been severely handicapped by the fact that the criteria of group and departmental effectiveness are only vaguely... defined ... and even less frequently are they measured with any degree of reliability.[23]

Few studies have been conducted that evaluate leadership training under controlled conditions with objective performance criteria; nor are disinterested studies done. Evaluation is often a subjective report by participants on their perceptions of how useful the program is. Informal comments and testimonials do not provide an independent measure of change in attitude or behavior, especially productivity.

One of the earliest research studies was carried out in 1951 by **Ralph Canter**. He evaluated a training program designed to increase cognitive skills (understanding) of supervisors. A posttest showed an increase in knowledge for trained supervisors, but subsequent surveys of subordinates on the job indicated no increase in morale attributable to training.[24]

In another study, mentioned earlier, conducted at the Ohio State research center, Fleishman developed a design and battery of surveys for measuring continued effectiveness of training; the LOQ and the LBDQ. These questionnaires, as indicated, measured the C and S factors from both the supervisor's and the subordinate's point of view. Although significant changes in C and S were found immediately after training, no effect was established when measured on the job. Fleishman concluded that "the training, however, did not produce any kind of permanent change in either the attitudes or behavior of the trained foremen."[25]

Later studies by **M. Gene Newport** and then **Lawrence Meyers** reported much the same thing—little or no effect of management training. Although trainees judged themselves as having changed in relation to training goals, significant others rated them as not having changed. Changes in awareness evidently were not translated into behavior.[26]

If there are immediate changes in behavior as a result of training, the evidence does not suggest that they are lasting changes. It does indicate that trainees do not maintain changes learned in the laboratory or classroom. If there is no immediate and direct reinforcement in the work environment, studies show that learned behavior will not continue.[27] Confirming these findings are studies that show that organizational climate can negate or overwhelm training when upper management reinforces behavior that is inconsistent with training.[28] Fiedler also stresses that the laboratory or classroom experience will be useful only to the extent that the situation is nearly identical to that present in the leadership training. He believes that training can provide an opportunity to "experiment with attempts to change the leader member relations. . . . Whether laboratory training can affect changes in the individual's leadership style is considerably more doubtful."[29]

According to Fiedler, it is more likely that we can seek effective leadership in business by altering aspects of the situation (such as designated power or group members) or by selecting appropriate leaders with styles that fit the particular situation, rather than trying to train someone to change their leadership or management style.

It is possible that changes in behavior do occur as a result of training but that the changes are not those that were specified in the program objectives, so that they are, therefore, overlooked in the search for manifest changes. Since these changes or consequences cannot be predicted, management consulting that employs training and the social science approach is itself not a science, even though the social and psychological theories it uses are scientific in the sense that they are based on laboratory research.

## RELATION OF THE MANAGEMENT CONSULTANT
## TO THE CLIENT COMPANY

A review of the literature reveals a variety of opinions about how the consultant is used in industry. The consultant is seen as a change agent, or as a diagnostician, or as a problem solver. The variety of consultant functions are suggested by the reasons why organizations use outside management consultants, by the factors involved in the selection of the management consultant, by criticisms of consultants, and by consultants' styles.

There are many reasons why business organizations hire management consultants. One of the reasons is that they feel they do not have the expertise necessary within their own organization. **Don Bowen** explains that with the rapid and unpredictable changes occurring the accepted maxim has come to be that "The only constant is change itself." At the same time, professional knowledge and skills are expanding so fast that even with the best of care it will be unlikely that an organization will have the "complement of in-house competencies when, where and in the quantity needed."[30]  This has led to increasing specialization among management consultants.[31]

Organizations are also prone to recruiting from professional staffs of major consultant firms to fill senior management positions rather than promoting from within the organization. This is done on the assumption that the consultants possess better expertise and experience than the company's own managers. Yet **John Miner** has examined this assumption by comparing corporate managers and management consultants on measures of motivation and mutual ability, both of which factors have been known to have some relationship to managerial success. He did not find a pattern of superiority among the consultants.[32] Good management talent was found equally in both groups. This does not mean, however, that specialized consulting firms in total do not possess a wider range of techniques and information than any one operating organization may possess.

Another reason for seeking consultant advice is to get an independent view. In an activity in which the judgmental element is high, "another opinion" is often sought by those concerned. The "credibility of an outside and independent perspective in the often internecine or interjurisdictional warfare and the personal and political antagonisms attendant to such disputes" is an important factor.[33] A third-party view may both be better than the judgments of more immediately concerned parties and have an acceptance that will facilitate action where there has been an organizational standoff.

The politics of a situation may also require bringing in an outside consultant, even when the expertise exists in-house, to give the impression of neutrality.[34] Others support the view that outside consultants should be brought in for politically sensitive issues or for top management reorganization or for changes in corporate strategy.[35]

There are those, however, who feel that the management consultant does not maintain the objectivity he is hired to provide. **James Kennedy** states that although the biggest advantage a management consultant brings to the client is his objectivity, this quality "erodes as the consultant gets to know the client better. While some indoctrination into company affairs undoubtedly helps, there comes a time when the consultant's blinders are almost as big as those worn by the regular employees."[36]

Others also claim that consultants are not any more objective than regular employees: they have to please the person who hired them. "Even outside consultants can't spit on the flag," comments **Walter Guzzardi**.[37] "External consultants can be either objective or tainted too. . . . They know which side their bread is buttered on."[38]

Management consultants are, in addition, described in an analogy to a physician. They are expected to diagnose, sort out causes from symptoms, prescribe remedies, and check back to see if their suggestions are being carried out.[39] According to **Nicholas Radell**, a good consultant should be an expert at recognizing and defining solvable problems. Management sometimes falls into the pitfall of "identifying and dealing with symptoms rather than with more basic, underlying difficulties."[40] This is where the consultant's experience and objectivity are real assets because they are not so involved with the company and they have been exposed to a number of similar situations in other client organizations in the industry.

### The Selection of a Management Consultant

According to Nicholas Radell, a vice-president of a leading management consulting firm, a subjective judgment must be made when selecting a consultant. "The only means available in minimizing the risks involved is to gain as much insight as possible into the consultant choices available."[41] He suggests that an organization should request a written proposal that clearly defines the objectives to be achieved, the end products that the consultant will deliver, an estimate of the time required to complete the project, the costs involved, and a list of the staff assigned. Radell feels that there is always a risk in selection because, "At the time a consulting engagement begins, not even the consultant can predict the substance of the product he or she will create and deliver, i.e., the conclusions reached and recommendations made."[42]

**Steven Brown** also recommends evaluating potential consultants by having them submit written proposals and then evaluating the costs and benefits.[43] Guzzardi sees an increase in the number of companies who are getting several bids before selecting a consultant for a project. "They invite three or four consulting firms to outline their approach before making any assignment and seek to have fees as far as possible fixed in advance. . . . The best results seem to come when management knows what the problem is, and sets down clear boundaries and objectives in advance."[44]

Both Brown and Radell emphasize manifest *presenting problems* both in consultant selection and in the clear manifest statement by the consultants of their own terms of reference; by implication, they deny the existence of latent meanings in the selection of problems.

Other difficulties may arise out of a lack of clear definition of what the consultant will do. Some consultants "insist that their professional responsibility ends when they have carefully analyzed a problem and have presented well-conceived recommendations to deal with it."[45] If the client does not have the means or knowledge to implement the recommendations without assistance, this could result in a worthless end product of consultation; or it could lead to inaction or less-than-adequate action.

When selecting a management consultant, many companies will go immediately to one of the top 10 or 15 firms, relying on reputation. More and more, however, companies are seeking out a number of smaller firms to reduce costs and/or to obtain the expertise needed in the increasingly specialized market. **Business Week** reports that "for their part, clients themselves show increasing willingness to forego one-stop shopping at a prestigious consulting firm in order to get a multidiscipled approach."[46] This has led to a proliferation of smaller and more specialized consultant firms. Companies may use several specialized consultants rather than one large firm.[47]

All of this discussion deals only with manifest problems and functions except in the suggestion by *Business Week* that a top firm offers prestige as well as multiple services.

### Criticisms of Consultants

One of the problems that occurs with the use of management consultants stems from the fact that management consulting itself has become a growth industry. The growing complexity of the world and of organizations has generated more and more work for consultants. At the same time it has also led to fragmentation in the consulting industry.

> Thousands of academicians and other professionals have capitalized on their technical expertise in fields such as transportation, productivity, data processing, and the behavioral sciences to establish successful individual consulting firms, which together are offering a serious competitive challenge to the biggest and most well-known names in the business.[48]

It is interesting to note that while academicians have always done consulting as a sideline, the practice has now reversed itself to the extent that teaching has come to supplement lucrative consulting practices. In places such as the Harvard Business School, faculty members with consulting incomes may be earning several times more than their salary from teaching.

Another aspect of the growth of the consulting firm is that the staffs grow quite large, which may lead to a dilution of the care and quality that have earned the firm its reputation in the first place. Only a few consultants at the top have the experience one expects, and pays for, with the top consultant firms. One way the consultant firm maintains its profitability is by bringing in new, inexperienced staff members who earn for the consulting firm far more than they are paid. While companies are paying for the experience of the senior members, "the fact is that ranking members of a big consulting house have many clients to serve and new accounts to worry over. They cannot give much time to any single client's problem; it just isn't economical for them to do so."[49] If a client goes to a big consulting firm he is not getting the top partners but one of the younger, less experienced members.

Radell explains that "consulting firms do not perform consulting engagements; individual consultants do. A client has the right to know who is going to do the work, who is going to manage the work, and who is going to be fully accountable for the successful completion of the work."[50]

Guzzardi provides an example of the problem as he severely criticizes consultants:

> In our instance, the executive's company has a good record of earnings, but he is troubled, let us say, by the loss of some competent young executives from one division. Unsatisfied by the explanation from within the ranks, he calls in a consulting firm of renown to have a look. A senior member of the firm responds, and, in brief and intelligent preliminary analysis, recommends an executive compensation study. . . . Impressed with the analysis and with the demeanor and experience of the senior consultant, the executive agrees to the study. The senior partner is seen very little around the company after that, and the youth of the consultants who actually do the work lifts a few company eyebrows.[51]

Another criticism of consultants is that they are continuously finding new problems, which perpetuates their business, and that sometimes in the process of "solving" problems, they create new ones. Guzzardi refers to them as "the men who came to dinner" and as masters of the "self-perpetuating sell."[52] No serious problems can be left unsolved for long, but even solutions proposed by consultants bring new problems in their wake. For example, after conducting the executive compensation study mentioned above, the program is implemented by the company. A solution seems to have been found to the problem until the consultant points out that there is another problem—which in effect he created. The compensation study that was done for one division has thrown top management out of kilter and, therefore, requires that an entire organization study be made to restructure the compensation system.

Part of the problem may be the *increasing specialization* of consulting firms. The narrower perspective, while providing more expertise in a particular area, tends to increase the possibility of creating problems in other parts of the organization. This occurs because no one looks at the ramifications for the company as a whole. By focusing attention on manifest problems, there may be a tendency to overlook underlying or latent problems.

Another problem with consultants is that there is no way to calculate the *fair price* of the consultant's advice. There is no guarantee of "quality of advice; there is no approved scale of fees; there is effectively no redress in the event of a botch-up."[53] **Rosemary Brown** cites some instances where the consultant, called in to cure a sick organization, wound up killing it. In one example, the cost of the consultant's services turned out to be almost a quarter of the company's annual profits and bankrupted the company.[54] Brown's discussion, suggests that management firms can make gross mistakes, but Brown's emphasis is on the fees and technical failure of the consultant's advice, not on the latent function of the advice.

Another example is that of a consultant firm that did good work for one large company but left "a string of embittered people behind. In effecting the savings that its gifted salesman promised for the client, the consultant left one senior survivor convinced that 'the impact on spirit has been devastating. This is a blow from which the (company) will never recover.' "[55]

Part of the problem, according to a 1979 *Business Week* article, is that consulting is an unlicensed, unregulated profession—one in which any person can hang out a shingle and adopt the label of consultant. There is a strong need for standards in an area where growth has occurred so fast that its overall performance standards have weakened. This assumes that consultants were better in the past and that the major problem of consulting firms is their technical inability to deliver on their promise.

A related problem of standards arises when there is a possible *conflict of interest.* Most consultants gain their expertise by working with several clients in the same industry. Thus they occupy a position of trust (many are asked to sign nondisclosure agreements covering technical processes). The temptation may be great to use knowledge gained from another company.[56] Some favor obligating the consultant to be certified or regulated in a fashion similar to the way that lawyers and physicians adhere to professional standards. In regard to conflict of interest especially, "by the very nature of the business, consultants who serve competitors are forced to play the role of both poacher and gamekeeper."[57]

It may be unrealistic to expect a consultant to have information that would help with another client in the same industry but to refrain from using it to his own advantage. The ethical problems suggested here assume that the unethical consultants defraud clients, that each firm is an entity, and that there is no collusion between consultant and individual representatives of the client.

Still more problems may occur because of the mistakes the consultant makes in working with the client organization. **William Reddin,** a well-known management consultant who specializes in organization development and conducts his own leadership-style program, has made a survey of consulting-management problems. He outlines nine errors that are commonly made with the client. The errors include: "initiating change from the bottom up, creating a change overload, raising expectations beyond what is possible, allowing inappropriate attachment, becoming trapped in one part of the organization, changing only a sub-system, mistakenly intervening behaviourally rather than structurally, losing professional detachment, and assuming that change is needed when it isn't."[58]

*The first error—initiating change from the bottom up—is a well-known mistake.* Reddin says that "when change agents tell me that they plan to attempt to change from the bottom up, I remind them of the military dictum that the penalty for mutiny is death."[59] He gives an example of what happened when he conducted a well-budgeted series of workshops for everyone except the very top managers. Although the first seminars were well rated by the participants, the top management team cancelled the budget after the first three sessions.

> What happened was that successive waves of managers with radically different ideas of how the company should be run were causing a tremendous disturbance, and we had not prepared the top team for dealing with it.
>
> I am frequently pressured by clients to make this error again. . . . The person who makes this request usually explains that the top man is too busy to attend a seminar, does not need it, or could simply read the book.[60]

Here Reddin accepts the principle of hierarchy and finds that consultants must work with the very top. The criterion of success is the retention of contracts.

*The second error involves creating more change in the organization than it can handle at one time.* A rigid or bureaucratic system will alter and undermine any meaningful changes if they are introduced too fast or if it is unprepared to handle them. A single, one-shot large-scale intervention is not likely to produce any change in such systems. Changes, he argues, should be introduced gradually and assimilated before any new changes are attempted.

*Reddin gives an example of the third error—raising unrealistic expectations.* He recounts the introduction of a participative goal-setting program—a **Management by Objectives (MBO)** approach. The top person in the organization decided to introduce the program by having everyone attend a meeting to discuss the MBO program. This was an immediate error, Reddin says, because "the top man's autocratic decision was hardly the way to introduce a participative approach, and the meeting raised expectations beyond the delivery point.[61] The people expected that the participative management style would be used immediately and in all areas. This was not top management's intent; and when in the next few months the budget and other key decisions were made in the usual autocratic way, the managers were disappointed and became disillusioned with the entire MBO program. If change had been introduced in a more limited fashion, it would have had a better chance of succeeding.

*The fourth error is what Reddin calls "inappropriate attachment" in the relationship of consultant to client.* Here the consultant forms a relationship that is inappropriate for maintaining the professional, objective approach. Reddin humorously recounts how he lost his effectiveness by being "seduced" by his client. He describes how he was invited by the chairman to dine with the board members at their country house training center:

> It was an epic meal and the vintage port flowed. The conversation was witty, and I had to lean on my limited classical education to keep up with the literary allusions. . . . My first error was to accept that invitation, and my next was to visit again in similar circumstances. It was a superb, if unconscious, seduction of me by the client. My role in this case became that of an intellectual, witty companion. My attempts to change it were met with difficulty.[62]

Here we have, perhaps, a truncated version of a latent function of consulting. It is truncated in that Reddin does not discuss how his social *co-optation* affected the manifest statement of consulting problems and his response to them.

*The fifth error also involved inappropriate attachment: being confined to one part of the organization rather than forming connections throughout.* As a result, the consultant's perspective may become too limited. This problem can be caused by the wrong type of entry into the organization. The entry may be through one individual, which limits access to information. Another aspect of this problem is entering too low in the organizational hierarchy or having contact with an individual rather than with the group. Reddin suggests that inappropriate attachment results in limited sources of information, limited diagnosis, and, therefore, limited recommendations. It also suggests co-optation and the inability to "sell" his recommendations to higher and wider levels.

*Changing only a subsystem is a mistake when there is mutual dependence or interdependence with other parts of the organization.* This might involve making changes in only one part of a division that brings it into conflict with the rest. Changing only a part of the organization may also bring disorganization where consistency would be more efficient. The example of bottom-up change, exclusive of top levels, would be another example.

*Intervening behaviorally when structural change is more appropriate is a more common error made by management consultants involved with organizations and management development.* For example, if a task group is having "personality clashes," it is all too easy to rush in with human relations skills training when, in fact, the problem is caused by a lack of definition of roles and responsibilities. Another example of this would be offering management training workshops to try to lower high turnover when the problem should be addressed through the compensation program. These may be technological errors, or they may be the result of consulting firm specialization; a firm specializing in human relations or skills workshops may be unwilling to recommend services it cannot provide.

*The error of becoming emotionally involved with a client is easy to make because the consultant's reputation and fees are at stake.* In becoming too concerned with having his project "succeed" in the client's view, the consultant may lose objectivity and professional detachment when associating too closely with the client: becoming concerned about being "liked" by the client, liking the client and becoming too personally involved, or accepting as "success" the client's praise without looking at the situation and all its ramifications. This error seems to imply the adherence to latent motives of some individuals in the client firm and a co-optation to the client's diagnosis, perspective, or interests. Reddin does not, however, expand on this.

*The last error Reddin discusses is that of introducing change when none may be necessary.* In the consultant's zeal for work or overenthusiastic assessment of his own ability, he may introduce a new way of doing something when the old way was satisfactory—or perhaps better. The consultant, not being as familiar with a particular company's functioning, may do great damage if he fails to heed the advice of knowledgeable people in the organization.

In summary, Reddin discusses how consultants may be co-opted as they work with clients, sometimes by the top, sometimes by lower levels, and sometimes by specialized parts of an organization. Some of his points suggest that co-optation in some form may be necessary to accomplish the changes in the organization. His last point suggests that a preference for certain types of diagnoses and recommendations—regardless of solution—may limit consultants' flexibility and, therefore, their effectiveness.

None of Reddin's cases report directly on the effects of co-optation by management officials on manifest diagnosis and recommendations. They do suggest, however, that management resistance is the greatest problem, and they suggest the necessity for the consultant to co-opt the managers.

Reddin has supreme confidence, with the exception of one case, in the value of his work. The only problem he presents is getting the opportunity to apply it to the total organization with the aid of the person at the top.

## Consultant Styles

Not much research has been done on the effects of the management consultant's style on the intervention process. **S. R. Ganesh,** while not addressing this issue explicitly, has at least begun to examine the consultant's style.[63] He interviewed some management consultants and defined an organizational consultant in terms of the activities he engaged in.

Ganesh contends that since it is the organizational consultant who facilitates the application of existing behavioral science to ongoing organizations, there is a need to understand individual consultants in terms of their styles, which influence their interventions. From interviewing 21 consultants, he arrived at two basic approaches: an emphasis on people and an emphasis on task.

The *people-oriented style* used by consultants involves an emphasis on individuals and groups. A concern for others' feelings and the relationship they have with each other and with the consultant is paramount. The people-oriented approach focuses on the people in the organization as the most important aspect of getting the organization to function well. The emphasis is on interpersonal relationships, which involve getting along with people, trust, and open communication.

The *task-oriented style* is more concerned with the task itself and the structure of the organization. Task-oriented consultants emphasize getting the job done, the systems within the organization, and the way work is structured. Task orientation focuses on systems of work and efficiency.

The various styles fall along a continuum from the most people oriented to the most task oriented. As one moves to the right on the continuum, there is less concern with personal or interpersonal issues and more concern with total organizational issues (see Table 1-2).

The people approaches consist of training and working with groups, working on personnel aspects, working with individuals, and working on both people and task approaches but emphasis on people.

Task approaches are working on task and structure aspects, working on information control and communications aspects, working on organizationwide goal setting, and working on strategy.[64] The way that the consultant carries out the assignment may vary depending on the approach and style employed. Ganesh identified elements of style related to *overall approaches* and to the *individual personality* of the consultant.

There are three elements of style related to overall approaches. The first is called *entry* and has to do with the way the consultant enters or comes into the organization. It encompasses the way the consultant makes contact with the client organization and the level or levels of management through which the consultant comes into the organization. The second approach element is the involvement of the consultant with the organization. This includes the period of time the consultant works in the organization, the dependency of the client on the consultant, and whether or not the consultant tries to build the internal abilities of the client organization so that they can continue to function well after the consultant leaves. The third element is the degree of change that is created by the consultant's intervention. This includes the type or amount of change that occurs and the object or systems in the organization that are involved in the changes.

There are also three elements of style related to the individual personality of the consultant. Ganesh calls these the *"person-related"* elements. The first of these elements has to do with the *role* that the consultant plays in the organization in which he works. The consultant may take one role, or he may play several roles, at one time or in sequence. The role that the consultant plays in interacting with various groups within the client system may vary. Some consultants become active members of their client groups, while others do not attempt to join at all.

The second person-related element involves the *relationship* that the consultant establishes with the client organization. The consultant and the client may interact on a formal or an informal

**TABLE 1-2**

**CONTINUUM OF CONSULTANT STYLES**

| Increasing Emphasis on People Variables | | | | Increasing Emphasis on Task & Structure Aspects | | | |
|---|---|---|---|---|---|---|---|
| Training and working with groups | Working on personnel aspects | Working with individuals | Working on both people and task aspects, but emphasis on the people | Working on task and structure aspects | Working on information control and communications aspects | Working on organization wide goal setting | Working on strategy |

***SOURCE:*** S. R. Ganesh, "Organizational Consultants: A Comparison of Styles," *Human Relations* 31 (1978): 23. Reprinted with permission.

basis that establishes the consultant's particular concern for the client's welfare. The consultant may also bring to his relationship with the client personal expectations for professional learning.

Lastly, there is the *power* element of style, which involves whether or not the consultant is aware of his own power (or lack of it) in the client organization and the type of power the consultant exerts—based on expertise, trust, position power.[65]

According to Ganesh, consultants using the people approaches tend to enter the organization at middle levels. Personnel consultants express interest in entry at top levels since "access to the top is necessary to introduce changes that affect the total organization . . . but are quite content to start lower down."[66] All the other approaches, including the task approaches, tend to enter at the highest levels because "the rationale for entry at middle levels appears to be the emphasis on improvement of individual and group functioning, whereas the rationale for entry at the highest . . . levels appears to be the focus on cultural change."[67]

The major differentiation between the people approaches and the task approaches seems to center on their **values**. These values underlie the type of approaches that are used by the consultant. The task approach is generated by values that Ganesh calls a **systematic relationship (SR) orientation**. Consultants with an SR orientation are usually involved with issues that affect the entire organization and in changes that affect the long-term patterns of work in the organization. The SR orientation is based upon working from formal power bases and using these to bring about desired changes in the total system. Consultants using the SR orientation avoid personal involvement in their relationship with the client. They attempt to maintain a detached perspective rather than getting involved in personal or organizational politics. They may, Ganesh concludes, be involved with an organization for a long period of time and develop a good working relationship with a concern for the client's welfare on a professional rather than a personal level.[68]

The **human relations (HR) orientation** usually involves personal, interpersonal, and group situations. The changes that are attempted are directed to individuals or groups that are parts of systems within the organization. This approach is focused on only parts of the organization and thereby limits the consultant's

involvement in the total system. This limitation, in addition to
the way these consultants enter the organization (usually
through personnel and training managers), influences the nature
of the changes they are able to bring about. Limited involvement
also fosters the need of these consultants to feel that they are
members in a client group. Although they come in as experts,
they work from a position of trust with the client. They profes-
sionally emphasize the interpersonal skills that lead to personal
relationships based on trust. These include facility at communications, getting along with others, and sensitivity to others
rather than impersonal objectivity.[69] Ganesh's descriptions of
consultants' styles will be used to characterize the consultants'
relationship to the company in the case study.

## Variety of Services Provided by Management Consultants

Management consultants with a social science approach often of-
fer several services to clients. In addition to providing assessment
and analysis of management problems, the consultant might also
design, market, and sell various management games, simulations, and programs. These "products" are based on academic social sciences and are derived from university research that has
been adapted for business. The university origin of the product
adds credibility and prestige, which help the consultant sell the
products to business client organizations.

The management consultant might sell his game or program
directly to the client, or, most often, he may actually conduct a
series of workshops for the client. Thus the management consultant frequently takes on the role of management trainer for the
client organization. In the management training workshops, a
variety of techniques, borrowed from the social sciences, may be
used. The particular techniques selected to achieve the desired
results may depend not only on the appropriateness of the techniques themselves but also on such conditions as the prestige or
reputation of the consultant and previous clients who can attest
to his effectiveness.

In this study the emphasis is on the management consultant
who specializes in a social science approach. This emphasis is
made because the author has worked as a consultant to business
and industry utilizing such an approach and is most experienced

with it. In addition, during the period of the case study, there were several management consultants with social science approaches working for the company, which provides material for comparisons and analysis.

## TECHNIQUES USED BY MANAGEMENT CONSULTANTS

Having discussed some of the ways management consultants are used, some attention will now be given to the techniques and processes utilized by consultants in the management training programs.[70] Consultants often use a workshop format for the management training programs. This format may include exercises, discussions, role playing, lectures, case studies, questionnaires, and additional participative techniques. Often the workshop starts out with an exercise designed as a warm-up technique, which permits the participants to relax and get to know one another. Thus the workshop utilizes a variety of techniques, usually in combination.

The workshop is designed to be a problem-solving or knowledge acquisition session in which trainees contribute ideas and learn from one another rather than by formal instruction. The program leader takes the role of the facilitator, asking questions, guiding discussions, summarizing, and drawing conclusions. This format is an experiential mode rather than a student-teacher mode. The presumed benefits of this format are that participants learn through independent discovery, develop their problem-solving ability, and are likely to have better retention of what they learn. It is alleged to be especially effective in attitudinal or behavioral change.

The *lecture* is a traditional method adapted from academic settings and one of the most popular techniques. The role of the consultant as instructor is that of "teacher," while the participant is the "student." It allows for presentation of a great deal of information in a short period of time to a large number of people, but it permits only the passive involvement of the audience in learning and therefore is presumably less successful in creating long-term changes in attitude or behavior. The lecture is usually used in conjunction with games, simulations, or role playing, all of which are used to demonstrate the dynamics of the theory presented in the lecture. Lectures, conversely, are used in workshops to provide the theory, origin, or scientific credence to the exercises or games being used.

The *case study method* starts with a written description of a management situation that includes one or more problems requiring analysis and a decision. Developed at Harvard, the case study method involves learning by individual participation and group discussion. For example, during a session on goal setting in a workshop, a case study may be presented focusing upon a manager and a subordinate setting sales goals. Through individual and, subsequently, group analysis and discussion, the group discusses how to set goals, how much the manager should prevail, and how much the subordinate should contribute. In this discussion individual managers are exposed to new ideas and the views of their peers.

Case studies are designed to provide realistic situations and complexity in a meaningful, active way. Possible drawbacks are that the session's success is highly dependent upon the ability of the instructor and that any one case may not be seen as relevant to a particular participant's job.

Still another technique is that of *management games and simulations*. These use competition in an artificial game situation to simulate organizational activities. It is an attempt to reproduce the dynamics of organizational behavior in a protected setting. For example, the game may deliberately not provide enough time or material for the participants to create and respond to stress as an approximation of pressures in the real business world.

Most games center around general management principles such as planning, decision making, leadership, and motivation. There are other management games that are more specialized for particular production, marketing, and financial problems. These often involve computer simulations.

A game such as the Wood Blocks might be used during a workshop on motivation. In this game participants build small wooden blocks in stacks to score points within a time limit. This game is used to illustrate—and allow participants to *experience*—the concept of need for achievement motivation.

A disadvantage of management games is that the game situation may be dissimilar to the participants' real situation. The competition among participants, while stimulating interest, may distort usual behavior (for example, adopting more conservative strategies to try to win). The amusement and fun of the play may distract too much from the desired lesson of the game. Here again, the successful use of this technique is dependent upon the ability of the instructor to gain participants' acceptance of the applicability of the "lesson" to the job. The advantages of games are that they may allow for the re-creation of real life work situations and that they create a high level of interest and participation.

*Role playing* and *psychodrama* are techniques used in workshops by consultants that derive directly from psychotherapy. In therapy they are used to help release unconscious drives and motivations when one begins to act out a scene with a protagonist (a father or spouse). In leadership workshops the influence of this technique is seen in the direct application and use of role playing and psychodrama in evoking self-awareness of one's unconscious motivations in work situations. For instance, in one leadership training program designed and conducted by consultants for companies, role playing and psychodrama constitute the major part of the program. A situation is given where two participants play their roles of subordinate, peer, or superior while the other group members are asked to observe their behavior.

From this situation they criticize the behavior of one of the role players in terms of the dimensions of dominance-submissiveness and warmth-hostility. These allegedly result in four styles of leadership: dominant-hostile, dominant-warm, submissive-hostile, and submissive-warm. A clinical attempt is made to categorize the role player's behavior in these terms with descriptive adjectives for each style. This is accomplished by observing, making notes, recording videotape, and reporting the conscious behavior that is presumably triggered by the unconscious motives and drives. The discussion is done individually and then by group consensus.

An attempt is also made to suggest alternative modes of behavior to improve the outcome of the relationship that may involve negative behavior or to counteract another person's behavior that has a negative impact on the work goals. A delineation of alternative strategies is undertaken to deal with each of the leadership styles. This provides a way to counteract or manipulate—perhaps on an unconscious level—the person exhibiting each style, supposedly to more work-productive ends.

Psychodrama is used in this program by having each person re-create a situation in which he experiences difficulty or conflict on the job. As the individual reenacts the scene, he relives a situation that he has undergone in the past that has made a strong impact on him. Most role players report they experience the same emotions they felt when the incident first happened. This provides an opportunity to work out unresolved conflicts and to develop new strategies to handle similar situations to produce more satisfactory outcomes.

Another example of the use of role play would be a situation where a company might be having many complaints of discrimination. The company might call in a consultant to conduct an affirmative action training program for their managers. As part of the workshop that the consultant would conduct for the company, role playing, psychodrama, and *role reversal* (where the individual takes the role of the other person or opposite position) may be used in handling prejudice. In attempting to change attitudes such as prejudice and stereotypic thinking toward minority groups, role reversal and psychodrama provide opportunities for changing identifications and evoking awareness of unconscious influences on one's own behavior.

*Sociometry* is still another technique borrowed from the social sciences that is used by consultants in management training workshops. Sociometry is applied in group exercises designed to make participants more aware of their unconscious feelings and behavior, that affect their interactions on the job, especially with their subordinates.

Sociometric choices are used to analyze coworker relationships. Each individual in the group is asked to choose others in the group with whom he would like to eat or work most. The individual lists his first three preferences among the group members in order. Each member may also be asked to indicate negative choices—for example, those with whom he would least like to work. The choices reveal the patterns of repulsions and attractions between one individual and others. Some relationships may be fulfilled and others only wished for, that is, desired but not actually occurring in the manager's life situation. The work group is then supposed to be arranged to give each person his choice of work partner, insofar as this is possible without violating the other members' choices.

Arrangement by sociometric preferences is advocated by some as the most satisfactory basis for a group because in groups of preferred members people are supposedly more secure and open. They can, therefore, function better. This method, then, can be used by consultants in forming groups during a workshop. Other factors, however, detract from this idea. There may be unconscious motivations behind a person's choices. Thus if a person relates to someone as he did to his father, this will influence the position in which that person will be chosen. Similarly, the choice made or the preference felt may be pathological or simply not helpful to total group functioning. In that case, it is argued, the choice should not be encouraged. Thus the sociometric method of forming groups, both on the job and in workshops, must—it is argued—be used carefully with the focus on optimal group composition in addition to individual preferences, however these criteria are actually defined.

Another sociometric exercise is called the **social atom**. This exercise is also used by consultants in workshops to make participating managers more aware of the subtle ways in which their unconscious feelings are perceived by the other people with whom they work. The exercise demonstrates the relationships between the subject and family members, between the subject and friends or enemies, or between the subject and others that may influence the subject. The participant is asked to draw triangles and smaller circles representing the men and women who are most influential in his life. By the positioning and relative size of these circles and triangles, much is revealed about the person's unconscious relationships. This may allow him to free himself and also to examine these relationships. It may make him aware of how he relates to his work group in terms of past or present family groupings. It has been noted that the leader of a group—in this case, the supervisor—is looked upon as a central authority figure. The supervisor becomes a surrogate parental figure to the subordinates.

Still another sociometric tool used by consultants is an exercise called the **social barometer.** In this exercise, words and phrases are read to the group, and participants are asked to stand in front of the number posted around the room (ranging from −50 through 0 to +50) that best expresses how they feel about the word. Some of the words or phrases used are *militant, Jesus*

*Christ*, and *gay liberation in teaching*. The participants then discuss why they chose the number they are standing in front of. This exercise may be especially helpful in an affirmative action workshop where prejudice and values are discussed. It helps to bring out unspoken feelings and assumptions that are made. By making the managers more aware of these, it is assumed that they will be able to react in a more positive way on their jobs.

A number of communications exercises that are used by consultants in communications workshops conducted for client companies are also derived from the social sciences. The exercises are designed to reveal to participants their unconscious behavior and its influences on their communication with others.

An exercise called the **Animal Game** is used to demonstrate the concept of self-disclosure, which is introduced during a lecture. Each person is asked to write down the name of the animal that best describes himself and one for each member of the group. They are then asked to reveal these names to the respective designee and to tell the group why they chose that animal. This begins the process of providing assessments of other people in a less threatening way than being told directly how someone feels about them. It also provides the individual with others' assessments of himself. One of the by-products of this exercise is a high degree of anxiety, which is noted at two times in the exercise. The first time occurs when the instructions are given; the second time is in evidence when there is a release of anxiety expressed by laughter during the "feedback" process. Another phenomenon that has been observed is that in a short period of time all of the participants gravitate toward one place in the room, forming a single group. It may be that they come together because surrounding themselves by others in the group serves as a source of protection or security.

This exercise encourages the development of group cohesiveness during the workshop by providing another opportunity for group identification. The revelation of feelings serves as an initiation to the group and as a way of sharing feelings. Similar exercises are often used in workshops as warm-up exercises.

Another communication exercise used in workshops is called **Three Images of Self**. The three parts of a person's self-concept are described to participants in a brief lecture. The exercise illustrates the concept and allows the participant to experience how other people see him. The lecture also points out that the self-concept (that is, how you see yourself, how others see you, and what you would like to be) is the most important part of effective interpersonal communication. This is because one's self-concept is conceived as influencing how a person behaves and how he is seen by others in unconscious as well as conscious ways.

Participants are made aware that a person may give certain impressions to others because of the way he feels about himself. The person may not realize that he is communicating these feelings to others and that his self-concepts affect the way he expresses himself, how he copes with angry feelings, or how open he is with others. The objective of the communication workshop is to make managers more aware of the ways in which they communicate so that they can be more effective in communication and in their relationships with subordinates, coworkers, and superiors on the job. Once they are aware of the unconscious factors in communication, they will presumably be better able to control their communication.

To further illustrate the self-concept as discussed in the lecture, the Three Images of Self exercise is used. The individual first describes himself in front of the group, and then the other people in the group describe their impressions of him. This shows the perceived self (how he sees himself) and the acting self (how others see him). The individual also discusses what he would like to become (the ideal self). The ideal self is greatly influenced by socialization factors. The different combinations of these three parts of the self-concept have varying effects on the communication between the individual and other people. If the perceived self is bigger than the acting self, the person is usually thought of as conceited or having delusions of grandeur. If the acting self is larger than the perceived, the person usually has an image of being insecure or lacking self-confidence. If the ideal self is much larger than the perceived, the person is usually viewed as being an unrealistic dreamer, whereas if the ideal self and the perceived self coincide, the person is viewed as complacent or self-satisfied. These influences on the communication between the managers and their subordinates are brought out with the aim of having the manager, through his awareness of these processes, improve communications on the job.

## NOTES

1. Elton Mayo, *The Human Problems of an Industrial Civilization* (New York: Macmillan, 1933).

2. Chester I. Barnard, *The Functions of the Executive* (Cambridge, Mass.: Harvard University Press, 1938).

3. Philip W. Shay, "Toward a Unified Discipline of Management," *Conference Board Record* 13 (June 1976): 64.

4. Abraham Zaleznik. C. R. Christensen, and Fritz J. Roethlisberger, *The Motivation, Productivity and Satisfaction of Workers* (Boston: Harvard University Press, 1958), p. 35; Rensis Likert, "Measuring Organizational Performance," *Harvard Business Review,* March-April 1958, pp. 41–50; Frederick Herzberg, *The Motivation to Work,* 2d ed. (New York: Wiley, 1959).

5. Loren Baritz, *The Servants of Power* (Middletown, Conn.: Wesleyan University Press, 1960), p. 173.

6. Dorwin Cartwright and Alvin Zander, eds., *Group Dynamics* (New York: Harper & Row, 1968).

7. William G. Scott, *Human Relations in Management* (Homewood, Ill.: Richard D. Irwin, 1962), p. 304.

8. Richard M. Hodgetts, *Management: Theory, Process and Practice* (Philadelphia: W. B. Saunders, 1979), p. 289.

9. Harold Koontz, Cyril O'Donnell, and Heinz Weihrich, *Management* (New York: McGraw-Hill, 1980), p. 664.

10. Robert Tannenbaum and Warren H. Schmidt, "How to Choose a Leadership Pattern," *Harvard Business Review,* May-June 1973, pp. 162–80.

11. Scott, *Human Relations in Management,* p. 411.

12. Ibid.

13. Baritz, *Servants of Power,* p. 184.

14. Edwin A. Fleishman, "Twenty Years of Consideration and Structure," in *Current Developments in the Study of Leadership,* ed. Edwin A. Fleishman and John G. Hunt (Carbondale: Southern Illinois University Press, 1973), pp. 7–8.

15. Abraham K. Korman, "Consideration, Initiating Structure and Organizational Criteria: A Review," *Personnel Psychology* 19 (1966): 354. Reprinted with permission of *Personnel Psychology* and the author.

16. Fred E. Fiedler, *A Theory of Leadership Effectiveness* (New York: McGraw-Hill, 1967).

17. Fred E. Fiedler, "Personality and Situational Determinants of Leader Behavior," in *Current Developments in the Study of Leadership,* ed. Edwin A. Fleishman and John G. Hunt (Carbondale: Southern Illinois University Press, 1973), p. 44.

18. Ibid.

19. Ralph M. Stogdill, *Handbook of Leadership* (New York: Free Press, 1974).

20. Fiedler, "Personality and Situational Determinants"; Lawrence K. Michaelson, "Leader Orientation, Leader Behavior, Group Effectiveness and Situational Favorability: An Empirical Extension of the Contingency Model," *Organizational Behavior and Human Performance* 9 (1973): 226–45.

21. Fiedler, *Theory of Leadership Effectiveness*, p. 6.

22. Ibid., p. 251.

23. Ibid., p. 251.

24. Ralph R. Canter, "A Human Relations Training Program," *Journal of Applied Psychology* 35 (1951): 38–45.

25. Edwin A. Fleishman, "Leadership Climate, Human Relations Training, and Supervisory Behavior," *Personnel Psychology* 6 (1953): 220.

26. M. Gene Newport, "Middle Management Development in Industrial Organizations," *Dissertation Abstracts* 25 (1963); Lawrence C. Meyers, "Some Effects of Facilitator Training on the Attitudes and Performance of People in Leadership Positions," *Dissertation Abstracts International* 31 (November 1970): 2962–63.

27. Scott, *Human Relations in Management*, p. 411.

28. Fleishman, "Leadership Climate"; Floyd C. Mann, "Studying and Creating Change: A Means to Understanding the Social Organization," in *Research in Industrial Human Relations*, ed. Conrad M. Arensberg et al. (New York: Harper, 1957), pp. 146–67.

29. Fiedler, *Theory of Leadership Effectiveness*, p. 201.

30. Don L. Bowen and Merrill J. Collett, "When and How to Use a Consultant," *Public Administration Review* 38 (September-October 1978): 477. Reprinted with permission.

31. "The New Shape of Management Consulting," *Business Week*, May 21, 1979, pp. 98–104. Subsequent quotations reprinted with permission of McGraw-Hill Inc.

32. John B. Miner, "The Management Consulting Firm as a Source of High Level Managerial Talent," *Academy of Management Journal* 16 (June 1973): 253–64.

33. Bowen and Collett, p. 477.

34. Robert E. Kelley, "Should You Have an Internal Consultant?" *Harvard Business Review*, November-December 1979, pp. 110–20.

35. "The Benefits of Doing Your Own Consulting," *Business Week*, May 16, 1977, pp. 62–66.

36. James H. Kennedy, "Management Consultants and Conflict of Interest," *Dun's Review*, March 1978, p. 117. Reprinted with the special

permission of *Dun's Business Month* (formerly *Dun's Review*). Copyright 1978. Dun & Bradstreet Publications Corporation.

37.  FORTUNE, Walter Guzzardi, Jr., "Consultants: The Men Who Came to Dinner," February 1965, pp. 138 ff. © 1965 Time Inc. All rights reserved.

38.  "Benefits of Doing Your Own Consulting," *Business Week*, p. 66.

39.  Nicholas J. Radell, "Optimizing the Management Consultant," *Data Management* 15 (August 1977): 132–36; reprinted with permission; Bowen and Collett, "When and How to Use a Consultant."

40.  Radell, "Optimizing the Management Consultant," p. 32.

41.  Ibid., p. 33.

42.  Ibid., p. 33.

43.  Steven W. Brown, "On Choosing a Management Consultant," *Arizona Business*, October 1975, pp. 9–14.

44.  Guzzardi, "Consultants," p. 238.

45.  Radell, "Optimizing the Management Consultant," p. 34.

46.  "New Shape of Management Consulting," *Business Week*, p. 101.

47.  Ibid., p. 99.

48.  Ibid., p. 99.

49.  Guzzardi, "Consultants," p. 238.

50.  Radell, "Optimizing the Management Consultant," p. 33.

51.  Guzzardi, "Consultants," p. 139.

52.  Ibid., p. 138.

53.  Rosemary Brown, "Two Cheers for Consultancy," *Management Today*, April 1980, p. 92.

54.  Ibid., p. 92.

55.  Guzzardi, "Consultants," p. 237.

56.  Kennedy, "Management Consultants," p. 117.

57.  Guzzardi, "Consultants," p. 237.

58.  William Reddin, "A Consultant Confesses," *Management Today*, January 1978, p. 67. Reprinted with permission.

59.  Ibid.

60.  Ibid., p. 67.

61.  Ibid., p. 67.

62.  Ibid., p. 68.

63.  S. R. Ganesh, "Organizational Consultants: A Comparison of Styles," *Human Relations* 31 (1978): 1–28. Reprinted with permission.

64.  Ibid., p. 7.

65.  Ibid., p. 8.

66.  Ibid., p. 8.

67.  Ibid., p. 9.

68.  Ibid., p. 22.

69.  Ibid., p. 22.

70.  Material from this section is drawn from the author's experience as a management trainer; from Sidney Mailick, *The Making of a Manager* (Garden City, N.Y.: Anchor Press, 1974); and from Scott, *Human Relations in Management.*

# T W O

# Theoretical Framework

A clarification of concepts and terms will be included since several concepts and theories will be used to explore the effects of management consultants and to describe the client organization.

The term *manifest function* is based on **Robert K. Merton's** definition meaning "those objective consequences for a specified unit (person, subgroup, social or cultural system) which contribute to its adjustment and adaptation and were so intended."[1]

The concept of *latent function* is based on Merton's definition of "unintended or unrecognized consequences of the same order."[2] In Merton's terms, these social functions refer to "observable, objective consequences and not to subjective dispositions (aims, motives, purposes)."[3] In this study *latent function* will be used to mean functions that are not publicly or officially recognized by the participants to the actions in question. They are objective in the sense that they are ascertainable; and to the extent that they are latent, the functions are not officially or publicly presented, discussed, or used as criteria for the evaluation of action and policy. In this sense *latent* means "private" expressions of what can become publicly accessible.

Latent meanings may, of course, become manifest in the process of discussion, conflict, and research. When this happens they are no longer latent meanings. They may also be manifest to some observers and participants but not to others. The process of discovering the latent meanings underlying manifest functions and their other latent functions is, of course, what consulting firms are supposed to do—that is, to discover hidden dimensions of a problem. It is the function of social science to lay bare these latent meanings and functions to make them manifest.

Since the consulting firm and the social scientist may have latent motivations, meanings, and functions of their own, the process of discovering latent meanings and functions is an indefinite one, or rather one of infinite regress, with no guarantee of final solution. Progress in the solution of manifest problems, in light of this inevitable contradiction in social science, is generally understood to consist of learning more about a given problem without necessarily finding a "final solution."

Social behavior is often viewed as irrational or dysfunctional when it does not or cannot attain its ostensible purpose. With the use of the concept of latent function, however, behavior can be seen to be functional indeed—although the function may be quite remote from its publicly stated or avowed purpose. The concept of latent function, as used here, may help to explain the paradox of the "discrepancy between the apparent, merely manifest function and the actual, which also includes the latent functions"—the unanticipated consequences of purposive social action.[4]

By applying this analysis to the work of management consultants for business organizations, the author will attempt to demonstrate how latent functions surrounding the consultant intervention interact with the manifest functions (the solutions of manifestly stated objective presenting problems) to create outcomes that often differ from those intended and thus to produce unanticipated consequences, at least from the standpoint of the statement of presenting problems and objectives.

Some of the most common and important behavior that underlies objective functions in organizations is that of *power acquisition*. As described by **Virginia Schein**, organizations are political environments in which the acquisition of power by officials and executives is a key motive.[5] Schein contends that power acquisition behavior is quite functional in that it may be sought for sound, *work-related reasons* or for achievement of individual or *personal* goals. Such power acquisition behavior seems unrelated to manifest functions because of the illusion that the organization is a rationally structured system built on a base of the division of labor, hierarchical flow of communications, and formal authority operated by individuals working toward corporate objectives. Because of this illusion, deceptive behavior is common in organizations. **Deceptive behavior** is defined as that designed to present a false impression or illusion (actions or appearances that present something that belies the reality of the situation).[6]

Both individual and work-related forms of power acquisition behavior exist in business organizations, but the extent to which both are deceptive varies with the nature of the organization and the kinds of power acquisition exhibited—personal or work related.[7]

With **Richard M. Cyert's** and **James E. March's** concept of the different types of organizations,[8] the frequency of deceptive behavior and power acquisition behavior can be explained. Using Cyert's proposed division of organizations into types according to the amount of slack that prevails in the environment, Schein argues that deceptive behavior is most likely to occur in *high-slack organizations*. She defines her basic terms:

> Low slack systems are those operating in highly competitive environments which require rapid and non-routine decision making upon the part of its members and a high level of productive energy and work outcomes in order to deal effectively with this environment. High slack systems on the other hand, are those operating in a reasonably stable environment requiring rather routine functioning and the maintenance of day-to-day activities in order to continue to operate in an effective manner. The record industry versus the insurance industry reflect the differences between low and high slack systems.[9]

The organization selected for this study is an example of a high-slack organization.

Schein proposes that there is more personal power acquisition behavior than work-related power acquisition behavior in high-slack systems, while there is less personal and more work-related power acquisition behavior in *low-slack systems*.

> In essence, vigorous competition in the environment will prevent managers from manipulating their activities in order to achieve their own personal ends and require more work-

related behaviors; whereas the absence of such competitive conditions permits managers to pursue their own goals without obvious disruption of the system.[10]

Schein further states that deceptive or covert strategies and tactics are more characterisic of personal power acquisition behavior and, therefore, that they are more pervasive in high-slack systems, which have noncompetitive environments that allow time for such activities.

In examining a high-slack organization in the case study to follow, the author will examine the effect of deceptive behavior on the consultant-client relationship.

The relationship between deception and personal power acquisition comes from the very nature of behavior that is designed to achieve personal, not work-related, outcomes. The illusion of the objective image of the company is used, however, to mask behavior designed to achieve personal objectives that are unrelated or even opposed to company operations. This requires the deceptive actor to use official expressions of organizationally related sets of intent and means to overlay his own covert or personally oriented intents and means. This overt mask hides the covert intents and allows the individual to "carry out personal intents incongruent with organizational objectives."[11]

Schein describes the (latent) functions that the deceptive behavior serves and explains how they may not necessarily be dysfunctional in their consequences for the organization—or at least for some individuals in it.

> While such covert intents and means of achieving personal outcomes, such as status and promotion, have been viewed as dysfunctional within organizations, these behaviors within high slack systems might actually be quite functional. More than likely, in low competitive environments, even high level managerial jobs are somewhat routine, thereby prompting the need for excitement through "political warfare." As part of this warfare, deception and intrigue add interest to the otherwise routine and even keel environment in which they are operating. Similarly, within organizations characterized by a stagnant, tenure-based promotion system, covert tactics designed to take over another subunit may, if successful, provide satisfying

rewards during the long intervals between organizational rewards.[12]

The political warfare also serves to foster the illusion that the organization is active, exciting, and competitive. Even in low-slack organizations there is deceptive behavior, although it is less common. Here, too, the deceptive behavior serves a purpose for the organization at large.

> What seems to be occurring in low slack systems is an organizationally-based deception as to how one operates effectively in the system. . . . Fast action and rapid decision making may require circumventing the formal systems so as to deal effectively with environmental demands. Hence, behaviors designed to develop power outside of one's formal authority so as to operate effectively—behaviors such as the development of influential contacts, trading favors, coalition formations, etc., become useful strategies for effective work performance.[13]

Behavior becomes deceptive to the extent that significant members of the organization delude themselves as to the way things really get done and fail to acknowledge the methods managers use to circumvent the system to get things done within it. The concepts of latent function and deceptive behavior will be used in the case study that follows to show how the management consultant operates in the organization, how the consultant and the outcome of consultancy are affected by these political activities in the organization, and how these factors help to bring about unanticipated consequences in the organization.

Other factors that affect the amount of slack and the way the organization functions are its **structure** and **size**. "Different sizes require different structures, different policies, different strategies, and different behaviors," according to **Peter Drucker**.[14] Although social organizations are too complex for neat quantitative formulas for size, "mass" always increases much faster than "surface."[15] The *law of surface and mass* is borrowed from geometry where the "surface of an object increases with the square of its diameter, while the mass increases with the diameter's cube."[16]

As a result there are sizes that "require a structure that is appropriate to performance and function, and sizes in which the structure needed to support the mass is inadequate or inappropriate and becomes an impediment. . . . Beyond a certain point the complexity becomes more than the structure—no matter how it is designed—can support."[17]

Drucker feels that size has a major effect on the strategy that the organization employs and vice versa. This is further complicated by the "big business may actually be a confederation of fair-sized or even of small businesses, each with its own strategies and its own markets."[18] In this case, the organization needs more than one strategy. The decentralized organization that is analyzed in the case study epitomizes this structure.

Size and complexity are primarily upper management's problems, in Drucker's view, because only they are involved in making the decisions related to the size and structure of the organization.

Size and structure are also affected by the growth of the organization. While the organization is expanding, it may be able to support a huge or complex structure. When the growth stops, however, that same structure may become inappropriate for the mass. Similarly, where the personnel in the organization have increased disproportionately to its structure and function, this contributes to high slack because there are more people doing the same or less work.

Another aspect of an organization's structure is the functions it serves. **William Greenwood** develops the concept of *functionalized staff* as referring to functional authority or organization.[19] He believes that this staff provides the benefits of having decentralization and centralization at the same time. Where there are geographically decentralized subunits that duplicate the basic operations, the necessary standardization and uniformity are achieved by having high-level staff personnel formulate policies and, sometimes, procedures. The subunits are decentralized except that they are responsible to the functionalized staff in the central organization.[20] Line and staff titles and authority are usually similar, but when there is a conflict between the two groups (line and staff), line supersedes staff authority until the conflict is resolved at higher levels of the organization. The organization that is analyzed in the case study exemplifies the centralized and decentralized structure that Greenwood describes.

Another way of viewing the structure and function of an organization is in terms of social form with:

    a. a set of individuals in offices,

    b. individual responsibility for definite tasks—functional activities—which are parts of a division of labor,

    c. an organizational goal to which the activities of the staff contribute, and

    d. a stable system of coordinative relationships, i.e., a structure.[21]

**Robert Weiss** defines an *office* as "a position in the organizational structure in regard to which role prescriptions exist."[22] The office also has a title, salary scale, and formal specification of duties. The tasks, or functional activities, of the organization that contribute to the organizational goals are allocated to offices and then become the responsibility of the individual who occupies the office.

The executives of the organization are expected to identify actively with the organization's goals, although they do not set the goals any more than other members, according to Weiss. He states that even when leaders leave, the organization maintains its direction. He feels that high-ranking executives have a special role in relation to organizational goals in that they are "responsible for the development of a program, a plan of action for the organization," as the means to implement goals.[23]

Weiss sees the organizational structure as an overall system of "coordinative relationships" that is relatively stable and changes only slowly over a period of time. If an individual leaves the organization or the office, his replacement will still retain most of the same relationships with the coworkers remaining. In Weiss's view the structure reflects the organization's division of labor and its method of operation.[24]

## ORGANIZATIONAL AND MANAGEMENT THEORY

Traditional management theory emphasized the formal nature and the process of management, which emphasized the exact legal and rigid delineation of functions and principles into such refined functions as planning, organizing, and controlling. Criticism of traditional theory is mainly concerned with its lack of responsiveness to the human or "people" issues. Much of the criticism comes from the behavioral scientists who claim that by following traditional management theory and goals we are creating "undesirable hierarchies of authority whose organizational structures are based primarily on principles of specialization and division of labor and processes."[25] Since these are dehumanizing, this leads to a conflict between the individual and the organization because it is a mistake to think of persons in totally economic terms.

**Chris Argyris** is one of the critics of traditional theory. He suggests that

> the formal organization and the administrative control system
> . . . may be viewed as parts of a grand strategy to organize human effort to achieve specific objectives or intended consequences; that this strategy is based on such principles of administration as specialization of work, chain of command, unity of direction and span of control; that the strategy creates a complex of organizational imperatives that tend to require individuals to experience dependence and submissiveness and to utilize few of their relatively peripheral abilities.[26]

Argyris claims that many of the problems organizations complain about—such as apathy, turnover, and emphasis on material rewards—are unintentionally created by the organization itself. The strategies the organization uses deny the individual's need for self-actualization and direct him toward dependence, subordination, and alienation. These unintended consequences are detrimental to both the individual and the organization.

To Argyris, organizations are open systems continually influenced by and influencing their environment. An organization of any human or social type is:

1. a plurality of parts

2. maintaining themselves through their interrelatedness

3. achieving specific objectives

4. . . . adapting to the external environment, thereby

5. maintaining their interrelated state of the parts.[27]

He does not explicitly maintain a distinction between latent and manifest functions but assumes the existence of manifest functions in maintaining specific (organizational) objectives. Latent functions, we infer, come about as the result of failure or ineffectiveness in maintaining organizational goals, integration, and an adaptive relationship to the organization's environment.

The way to examine an organization, according to Argyris, is to look at how it is functioning in terms of the science of values (*axiology*). An *axiologically good organization* fulfills the essential properties of its definition (above).

The only way to improve organizational strategies so that they serve both the individual and the organization (and Argyris is not too optimistic that this is possible) is to move toward the axiologically good organization (see Table 2-1). This, in our terms, would be the achievement of unity between manifest and latent function.

According to Argyris, individual mental health—as it is currently defined by psychologists—is consonant with his axiologically good organization. The healthy individual strives to be self-responsible and self-motivated and to decrease compulsive and defensive behavior, and so on. Individuals who are not in an environment that allows for healthy functioning can cause deterioration of the organization by apathy and defensiveness, which can lead the organization to become rigid and inflexible and thus unable to meet the competitive challenges of the present socioeconomic system.[28] Thus Argyris axiologically assumes that the healthy individual and the healthy organization are axiologically intertwined.

For Argyris the organizational structure is composed of a series of strategies to achieve specific objectives. The best strategy will, therefore, optimize activities to achieve the organization's objectives, maintain the organization, and help it adapt to the environment. Individual mental health and psychology are subsumed under organizational objectives.

## TABLE 2-1
## AXIOLOGICALLY GOOD AND NOT-GOOD ORGANIZATION

| Not-Good Organization | Good Organization |
|---|---|
| One part (subset of parts control the whole) | The whole is created and controlled through interrelationships of all parts |
| Awareness of plurality of parts | Awareness of pattern of parts |
| Unable to influence its internally oriented core activities | Able to influence internally oriented core activities |
| Unable to influence its externally oriented core activities | Able to influence externally oriented core activities |
| Ineffective problem solving | Effective problem solving |
| Nature of core activities influenced by the present | Nature of core activities influenced by the past, present, and future |

*SOURCE:* Chris Argyris, "The Integration of the Individual and the Organization," in *Social Science Approaches to Business Behavior*, ed. George B. Strother (Homewood, Ill.: Dorsey Press, 1962), p. 61. Reprinted with permission.

Argyris believes that the pyramidal structure of the past needs to be modified because its theory assumes that individual self-actualization is not relevant to effectiveness, whereas Argyris's model asserts it to be critical. In the future there is a need for flexibility in selecting strategies to ensure that the one that best fits the situation is used. Argyris believes, however, that it is not possible to create an organization where the individual's needs and organizational demands are completely consonant; but we should move toward the best form of compromise.[29] Yet, for him the ultimate criteria of effectiveness are always organizational objectives.

**Fremont Kast** agrees that there is a conflict between the organization structure and the satisfaction of the needs of individual workers. The U.S. economic system has been very successful, by and large, in meeting basic physiological and safety, but not higher, needs. While major firms have substantially met Maslow's lower-order needs, there is a tendency to undervalue the higher-level needs. "These have assumed a much more im-

**TABLE 2-2**
**ORGANIZATIONAL AND PROFESSIONAL ROLES**

|  | Organizational Role | Professional Role |
|---|---|---|
| Goals | Short run—immediate results | In-depth research—exhaustive testing |
| Control | Bureaucracy—management | Autonomy—colleague |
| Incentive | Organizational advancement—administrative duties | Professional success—professional activities |
| Influence | Executive authority—legitimacy from mandate attached to office | Expert authority—legitimacy based on competence |

**SOURCE:** William Kornhauser, *Scientists in Industry* (Berkeley: University of California Press, 1962), p. 12. Reprinted with permission.

are increasingly subjected to bureaucratic control. Thus tension is constantly created between the demands of the organizational role and the demands of the professional role. The built-in strains revolve around goals for professional work, controls for professional work, and the incentives and influences of professional work. Table 2-2 summarizes the tensions.

Kornhauser felt that the constant tensions between the requirements of the organization and professional standards result in a more effective organizational structure. This is largely the outcome of the expansion of professional services more and more into industry and the professional's dependence on industry's resources. Yet while Kornhauser argues against the complete integration of the employee within the organization, he saw the conflict as occurring between the manifest goals of two kinds of organizations and the resolution as lying in more effective organizational behavior. In such an analysis, what we have called latent functions are simply the by-products of unsolved problems. The struggle is between two sets of public roles, not between individuals or within individuals. Individuals as individuals are not relevant in this analysis except as disrupters or deviants of role-defined behavior.

**Alvin Gouldner** has another way of looking at the strains between organizational and professional roles. He refers to Merton's *cosmopolitans* and *locals* as the bearers of two types of latent social roles in organizations.[36] There may be differences between the two in reference groups and in values that conflict with those prescribed by their organization. These roles involve three variables: loyalty to the organization, commitment to professional skills and values, and reference group orientation.

> Cosmopolitans: those low on loyalty to the employing organization, high on commitment to specialized role skills, and likely to use an outer reference group orientation. Locals: those high on loyalty to the employing organization, low on commitment to specialized role skills, and likely to use an inner group orientation.[37]

Thus a local would be the "company man" or a professional who has taken on the values and goals of the organization above his professional values, while the cosmopolitan would be the professional who maintains professional standards and is oriented to outside values. Here, too, latent functions and meanings are the product of competing manifest functions.

**Loren Baritz** sees the same pressures applied by organizations to social scientists.[38] Whether employed or consulting, Baritz states strongly that social scientists have succumbed to organizational demands to the detriment of their professional standards. He feels that social scientists have been all too willing, in the name of objectivity, to go along with industry's demands. Baritz fears that the body of knowledge that has been developed in the social sciences will be used for the economic gain of business without consideration for individuals.

Baritz believes that the ability to control human behavior through complex and subtle means is a powerful tool that has been sold to business by the social scientists.

> Especially through the use of group pressures has management shoved its people into line. . . . Through motivation studies, through counseling, through selection devices calculated to hire only certain types of people, through attitude surveys, communication, role-playing and all the rest in their bag of schemes, social scientists slowly moved toward a science of be-

havior. Thus management was given a slick new approach to its problems of control.

Authority gave way to manipulation and workers could no longer be sure they were being exploited. . . . Many industrial social scientists have put themselves on auction . . . and the industrial elite have bought their services.[39]

Baritz also believes that the social scientist has lost his professionalism without realizing it. ". . . Because he accepted the norms of the elite dominant in his society [industry], [the industrial social scientist] was prevented from functioning critically, was compelled by his own ideology and the power of America's managers to supply the techniques helpful to managerial goals."[40]

Baritz contends that their very position in industry forced the technician role on the industrial social scientists because they were hired by management to solve specific problems and thus had to produce according to their employers' needs.

**Matthew Radom**, on the other hand, disagrees completely with Baritz about the function of social scientists in industry.[41] He conducted a study of 462 social scientists employed by business and found that they felt they were not compromising their professionalism. The social scientists in his study felt that they maintained their autonomy to a large extent. Radom also challenged Baritz's claim that the social scientist is exploited by industry. He contends that because social scientists work closely with executives and top management—unlike the physical scientists—they contribute to the decision-making process; therefore, they are better able to accept the resultant organizational goals. By influencing the organization's goals, they are able to make them compatible with their professional goals.

Radom also disagrees with the idea that professionals in private enterprise are concerned with colleague authority. His findings show that they look to their immediate supervisor for approval and success rather than to their colleagues or peers outside or inside the organization.

He asked the social scientists in his survey how they felt about Baritz's statement that they are paid servants of industry. He found no evidence to support Baritz's contention that social scientists are willing to do industry's bidding—those in the survey disagreed with Baritz's statement. Note, however, that the evidence Radom presents is based solely on self-perception and attitude surveys—self-reports. It may well be that the social scientists he studied are not aware that they are acquiescing to their employers or that they do not want to admit, even to themselves, such a role; such an admission would be a violation of their manifest professional standards. The pressures for compromise may be subtle and easy to rationalize. On the other hand, it is possible that Baritz exaggerates and that the contributions of social scientists in industry are generally helpful. In this controversy there are no simple answers; however, the case study offers some evidence that favors Baritz's views.

Radom seems to be saying that the conflict between individually internalized professional goals and organizational goals is not inevitable. By making a contribution to organizational goals, Radom feels, social scientists are able to control their work environment and to make the organizational goals congruent with their professional standards. They have the best of all possible worlds.

## SOCIAL SCIENCE THEORIES ADAPTED BY MANAGEMENT CONSULTANTS

Major theories adapted by management consultants with social science approaches will be examined as to the basic theory, pertinent research, and ways they are adapted by management consultants. There are several theories that are used by management consultants, primarily among those consultants with the social science approach who are involved in management development and training. These theories form the basis of many management training programs that are designed and sold by consultants to clients in industry.

**Abraham Maslow,**[42] a psychologist, proposed the theory that every person is striving to satisfy certain needs that can be classified into five levels based on a priority hierarchy (*need hierarchy*):

1. Basic needs (physiological),
2. Safety and security needs,
3. Love and belongingness needs,

4. Esteem and status needs, and
5. Self-actualization.

According to Maslow, when the lower needs are satisfied, the person is then motivated by higher-level needs. Self-actualization is only attainable after the other, lower-level needs are relatively satisfied.

Maslow's theory of needs has been adapted by social scientists who work as consultants as a means of stimulating the motivation of workers in business. Since management is highly interested in motivation leading to increased productivity, Maslow became quite popular beginning in the 1950s when the emphasis turned from monetary to other types of incentives. Maslow was not theorizing from experience in the world of work, however, nor was he concerned with the variety of ethnic groups that are now found in business. His theories are still used—but often in a modified form—by consultants who develop their own management training programs as the basis for motivating employees.

**Frederick Herzberg**[43] was one of the social scientists and consultants to take Maslow's need hierarchy and apply it to the work setting. According to Herzberg and his research, people are not satisfied or motivated on their jobs unless they have the opportunity to satisfy higher-level needs. These opportunities are provided by the content of the work itself (if it is interesting), responsibility, challenge, and the opportunity for advancement. Other factors, such as pay, working conditions, and coworkers, do not really motivate, according to Herzberg. These other factors keep people from being more dissatisfied with their jobs.

Both Maslow's and Herzberg's motivation theories are taught by consultants in management training sessions on motivation. When designing their own programs to sell to clients, consultants have also used Maslow's and Herzberg's theories to explain the motivation that accompanies leadership styles. Herzberg himself has been a consultant to industry where he developed a system called *job enrichment* for restructuring jobs to fit his motivation theory. His system has been implemented in large companies, including a major utility.

Another motivation theory that has been used by consultants is the *social motives theory* of McClelland.[44] **David Mc-Clelland**, in his research at Harvard University, identified three social motives as being especially important in the work environment: the *need for achievement*, the *need for power*, and the *need for affiliation*. All are related to managerial effectiveness. Initially, he proposed that effective managers had a profile that was high on need for achievement only. Now, however, he has established that other profiles are also effective. For example, an effective manager may be high on power and achievement needs.

Much of the organizational climate work that is done by prominent management consultants is based on McClelland's concepts of social motives. *Organizational climate* is the employee's perception of the work environment. McClelland's organizational climate surveys differ from other organizational surveys in that they are based on those factors that are related to effective performance, while such climate surveys as Likert's are based on measures related to job satisfaction. Organization climate studies have become accepted ways of trying to evaluate motivation and increase organizational effectiveness. They are often used by consultants as part of a *management audit* to help assess where organization problems are.

Disciples of McClelland who had worked with him at Harvard have started their own consulting firms and have applied his theories to industrial settings. These firms use social motive theories as the basis for their organizational climate surveys, motivation workshops, and other management training programs that are sold to their business clients. For example, motivation workshops may include lectures explaining McClelland's motivation theory, exercises in how to recognize these motives in subordinates, and action plans for using these ideas on the job.

Another area where social science theory has affected the work of management consultants has been in the influence of *psychoanalytic theory* on management training. Since much of management training takes place in small groups, there are many psychoanalytic influences stemming from Freudian theory applied to group behavior. Freudian theories are used to encompass both individual and group functioning. The group focus used by these consultants includes group exercises, group dynamics, and leadership styles.

One of the rationales for the extensive use of group work by management consultants who conduct workshops is that positive influences are believed to be gained from group work based on the psychoanalytic concept of the family, the first group in the individual's development. Family groupings are assumed to be the prototype for later group relations, so that a person is assumed to bring unconscious and conscious emotional attitudes to whatever group situation he is in. The number of groups a person is involved with expands as he develops, including the work group, but his orientation to others changes very little.

Groups can promote many positive effects, but they can also induce emotional regression. When properly used by the consultant, the group experience can further the individual's growth or learning (this is the basis for sensitivity sessions or T groups). Leadership training conducted by consultants attempts this. For example, in a permissive or supportive climate, the individual might be led to experience less anxiety and less need to cling unduly to his defensive patterns. He may become more receptive to new ideas or experiences and influences prompted by other members of the group. This is especially necessary when the consultant is trying to promote attitude changes in workshops.

One exercise that makes use of the group is that called the **Fallout Shelter**. This exercise might be used as part of an Equal Employment Opportunity (EEO) program that has been requested by a client. As part of the EEO workshop, the consultant might use this exercise to make participant managers more aware of their unconscious prejudices, their norms, and their values. The exercise is designed to make conscious and unconscious prejudices and stereotypes the object of self-consciousness and evaluation. Participants are told that they are fallout shelter wardens and that they must choose six people out of ten survivors to enter the fallout shelter. Each trainee first makes his own choices, and then the group works to achieve a group consensus. In addition to the examination of how groups function in influencing individuals to change their choices (peer pressure, compromise, and so on), the discussion of why certain people are excluded from the shelter brings out the unconscious prejudices and assumptions held by the respective group members. There may be a lack of identification with particular ethnic groups or scapegoating of others because of the trainee's own frustrations. They may use defense mechanisms or projections, or they may dislike others for what they are not but would like to be.

Another reason for spending time in small groups during workshops is that through the development of group feelings an opportunity for personal growth is provided. In an atmosphere of support and trust, the energy used in unnecessary defenses and inhibitions can be redirected toward ego development. The group, it is argued, encourages growth and stimulates the accumulation and release of blocked psychic energy.

Because cohesive groups are believed to work together better, both in the workshop and on the job, consultants try to foster group cohesiveness by providing opportunities in the group for (1) promoting group member identification by competition against other groups, establishing identification against rivals; (2) working on a common task or sharing common interests, promoting identification; and (3) transference, which may resolve emotional dependency especially in relation to authority through leader-member relationships.

In the group situation, individual narcissism extends to the group from pride in self to pride in group. The need for protection or support is fulfilled by group members. Group relations are influenced by the individual's ego development as well as group composition, norms, and climate. Groups are also encouraged by the consultant's conducting team building activities and management training workshops to promote receptivity to new ideas and to give managers insight into their relationships with workers on their jobs.

There are many psychoanalytic influences in the leadership workshops conducted by management consultants. One of the unconscious processes that Freud emphasized in groups is that of *transference*. Transference, the displacement of parental image onto a person in the current environment, may be strong when repressed drives seek expression. Instead of remembering the past, the individual unconsciously tries to relive his experiences in a more satisfactory manner. This is part of emotional dependency, and it is in evidence frequently in relation to authority. Its expression is likely to emerge in a group setting, particularly in relation to the leader. It is important for the manager to understand the leader of a work group in his job setting. In a group the "individual is brought under conditions which allow him to throw off the repressions of his unconscious instinctual impulses."[45] In the workshop, consultants discuss leadership styles that are used by managers in terms of dependence, creativity, initiative, and the emotional maturity of workers as members of the group. The leader is viewed as an important figure in the group for many reasons, including one cited by Freud:

> The individual gives up his ego ideal and substitutes for it the group ideal as embodied in the leader. . . . In many individuals the separation between the ego and the ego ideal is not very far advanced; the two still coincide readily; the ego has often preserved its earlier narcissistic self-complacency. The selection of the leader is very much facilitated by this circumstance.[46]

Although Freudian theory is not explicitly taught during the workshops, the implication and effects of his theories are very much present in leadership-style materials. As different leadership styles are presented and explained in lectures and group sessions, the effects on the group members are pointed out.

The dependency of subordinates or group members is a common complaint made by managers to the management consultant. The reasons for dependency—according to the psychoanalytic theories—are that along with identifications and transferences to the leader there may be a displacement of ego and superego functions onto the authority figure (leader or supervisor). This encourages emotional dependency and susceptibility to group influence. Research is cited to demonstrate the influence of the authority figure: the supervisor is always seen as a parental—that is, authority—figure no matter what his age. The degree of group dependence may vary according to the prestige of the leader, the kind of group setting (democratic or authoritarian), the type of leadership available, and the individual personality.[47]

The need to be able to choose the most appropriate leadership style for a particular situation or group is stressed during the workshops. Where there is a prevalence of authoritarian style, the disadvantages of its constant use are explained in terms of the dependency of group members and the lack of opportunity for development. With continual authoritarian leadership, group members, it is argued, lose their individuality because they must conform. No variation in responses (criticism or disagreement) is permitted, discouraging creativity. Individuals with weak ego development may actually seek out autocratic leaders because they want to satisfy their dependency needs. These issues are brought out during the workshop because it is believed that if the supervisor is aware of these possibilities, he can either avoid problems or understand ones that do arise.

## THEORETICAL DISCUSSION

The development of modern technology and administration in its scientific, technical, legal, administrative, organizational, financial, sales and marketing, and personnel ramifications has become vastly complex, specialized, and technical on industrywide national and international levels. As a result no one business firm is likely to have all the scientific or specialized knowledge of the specific operations needed to cope with the vast variety of internal and external "environmental" problems that an individual company faces in the course of its routine operations. Moreover, these routine operations are subject to "deroutinization" as a result of technological change, economic competition, legislation, and other external and internal changes within or around specific firms. Included are industrywide changes in the way companies are managed.

Consulting firms based on specific specializations in one or more aspects of industrial or corporate management are likely to have—or to promise—specific, specialized knowledge, techniques, information, and training in these areas. The consulting firm is likely to have industrywide experience in an area or aspect of management, while the client firm, focusing upon its routine operations, may have a more narrow focus and may be less sensitive, in the short run, to changes and developments in industry as a whole. Moreover, concern with specific problems and internal differences that underlie *presenting problems* may limit the firm's sense of objectivity about those problems. The management consulting firm may thus be asked to provide not only specific technical and administrative solutions to technical problems but also a sense of "objectivity" based on industry-wide experience. In addition, it may be asked, at least tacitly, to adjudicate differences of opinion or conflicts within the business organization.

The consulting firm achieves entry via the consulting assignment on the basis of a presenting problem, which we have noted may be of many orders: technological, administrative, and knowledge- or need-requiring. The definition of the presenting problem is made by particular executives of the organization's management who have the authority to request or initiate the employment of consultants by subcontracting to an outside consulting firm. The presenting problem may be due to actual, objective, manifest problems of the organization or to underlying, latent problems that may not be apparent to those who define the presenting problem. These may be disguised from the consulting firm or from some other significant members of management and its board of directors. The consulting firm, in accepting the assignment, may accept the problem on its manifest level or seek to ascertain if there is another problem at the latent level that is the source of the organization's immediate need.

Manifest problems may include:

1.  Finding means of cutting costs or increasing productivity, including technological and capital development;
2.  Discovering ways of streamlining the administration of internal operations, including fixing managerial accountability;
3.  Increasing management and employee morale;
4.  Providing executive and managerial training;
5.  Complying with newly created laws;
6.  Defining new goals for the corporation and devising new plans to achieve these goals; and
7.  Recruiting executives to operate new functions and replacing executives who are departing either through retirement, turnover, or lack of ability.

Latent problems may be entirely based upon or entangled with the manifest presenting problems, or they may be entirely different. These latent problems may include:

1.  The attempt of one group within management to gain greater influence or control over the organization, using a consulting firm's rec-

ommendation as a device for gaining such ascendancy; this includes the adoption of new techniques to which only one group has or may have access;

2. The attempt of the organization to purge itself of personnel who employ outmoded practices, policies, and techniques.
3. The attempt of the top elite to resolve conflicts and differences within the executive elite by obtaining an "objective" judgment from outside experts—the consulting firm;
4. The attempt of top executives who define the presenting problem to use management consulting to forestall criticism of the firm both from dissenters within the organization or from outsiders, especially government agencies;
5. The attempt of management to use consultants to delay the solution of an otherwise pressing problem or to establish the claim that no problem exists; and
6. The attempt of management to use consultants to advance an image of the organization as modern, up-to-date, and in the managerial "swim" even though no manifest problems exist.

This discussion of problems is based upon the fact that most corporations—like most other social organizations—are complex, divided, and often marked by conflict and a continuous struggle for control, mobility, positions, prestige, and other personal and group advantages. The struggle usually affects all manifest technical and objective operations of the organization and is sometimes, but not always, inseparable from these operations.

The consulting firm is thus most often asked to deal with both manifest and latent problems, but it deals with them at the manifest level. That is, the consulting firm will usually be asked to present its findings, recommendations, report or diagnosis, and its implementation scheme in terms of manifest and objective statements of the problem. Yet it must face the possibility that the presenting problems are unwittingly or wittingly designed to cover up latent problems. In this latter case, the consulting firm presents the manifest "objectives" as solutions to hidden, latent problems that are disguised in objective presentation.

In some cases, if the problems are purely technical, these findings may in fact only apply to manifest technical issues; but even when consequences of the recommendations and implementation are technical changes, those personnel who are not equipped to adapt to technical changes are likely to resist them, and those who feel they can adjust to them or even supervise their introduction (or are above them) will be likely to accept or push for their adoption.

The consulting firm that is aware of these complications, it is hypothesized, will have to develop strategies for handling them. In the process of accepting or rejecting an assignment, they may at some level be aware of possible imperfections in the definition of the presenting problem and may reject assignments on the basis of their manifest unreality. The consulting firm, on the other hand, may be aware that the problem presented by the client is not what is really needed; yet the client may not be willing to do anything other than what they state is needed. For example, the consultant may be called in and asked to conduct a management training program because the client feels this will reduce turnover among supervisors. The consultant may see that the real problem is that the client is not competitive in its salary scales. Unless the client is willing to review their salary administration policies, the consultant may turn down the assignment, or he may accept the assignment to reeducate the client.

Consultants may accept the presenting problem and, as a deliberate decision, confine themselves to it, even if they sense that the problem is manifestly unreal. They may, alternatively, accept the assignment and attempt to modify images of the presenting problem in the process of negotiation over the definition of the presenting problem, or they may attempt to redefine the problem in the course of their work.

Once the assignment has been accepted and the consulting firm gains additional information by exposure to the organization and other executives, it may permit its recommendations to be influenced by its study and experience in the organization and its relative co-optation by various factions within the organization. It may also be influenced by a desire to avoid conflict with one or more parties or factions or by a desire to continue its relationship with the firm in the future, regardless of the present assignment; or it may fail to perceive the underlying latent problems.

Its acceptance of the assignment may also be based either on a lack of technical and managerial knowledge sufficient to deal with the problems or on a lack of time and personnel or funds to permit a realistic study.

It is recognized that the consultant must, at least on a public level, present his work in terms of some statement of manifest, objective managerial science since his training in managerial science and his claim to objective expertise are the basis of his influence.

As a result of all these dynamics, it is hypothesized that the final recommendations or implementations usually reflect latent meanings that are apparently related to managerial theory or social sciences. At times, however, the presentation of findings will be based on other than the stated manifest problems that were presented to initiate the work and will be accepted.

At still other times, the presentation of findings other than those based on presenting problems will generate a whole new series of problems, conflicts, and troubles that were unanticipated in the original problems.

Sometimes the mere presentation of recommendations may generate new problems and conflicts; at other times the attempt to implement recommendations may reveal new, unanticipated problems that may be more serious than the original presenting problems. These four ways that latent meanings intrude upon manifest presenting problems constitute the specific focus of the study. This work is thus a study of the politics of management consulting, of the pressures and conflicts that affect a consulting firm while it works in the organization and that often influence its recommendations. It is also a study of the unanticipated consequences that ensue from management consulting.

In summary, then, Chapters 1 and 2 have given a brief history and background of the development of management consulting, a review of the literature that presents the theoretical framework for the consultant's relationship to the business organization, and a theoretical discussion of the politics of management consulting.

This study will henceforth focus on the manifest (intended or apparent) and latent (unintended or covert) effects of consultants on the organizations for which they are employed. The heuristic hypothesis is that although the consultant is hired for specific problems, in solving these problems he often aggravates other problems in the organization or produces new ones.

The theoretical discussion examines the possible ways that the consultant can create as many problems as he solves in the organization. The focus is on the covert behavior between the management consultant and members of the client organization since there is a tendency for the consultant to be influenced by the organization's managers even though he may attempt to use his professional knowledge to change the organization. Managers involved in factional intrigue within the organization attempt to co-opt the consultant and draw him into their partisan activities.

The theoretical framework takes into consideration the political behavior that managers engage in and that often affects the consultant's intervention. The organizational and management theory section describes the conflict created between the individual and the organizational goals. This conflict extends to the social scientist, whether he works for the organization as a regular employee or as a consultant. There is conflict, too, between the consultant as he tries to carry out his professional assignment and the goals of the manager who runs the operations of the organization. The political behavior that is often generated as a result of these conflicts may affect the outcomes of the consultancy.

Social science theories, often used by management consultants, give the organization new techniques with which to manage their employees. With the growth of social science theories of management, theories of motivation and leadership have had tremendous effects on organizations. Many of the techniques borrowed from the social sciences are employed in management training problems that are designed and conducted by management consultants.

## NOTES

1.  Robert K. Merton, *Social Theory and Social Structure* (New York: Free Press, 1968), p. 117.

2.  Ibid., p. 117.

3.  Ibid., p. 78.

4.  Ibid., p. 118.

5.  Virginia Schein, "Examining an Illusion: The Role of Deceptive Behaviors in Organizations" *Human Relations* 32 (1979): 287–95. Reprinted with permission.

6. Ibid., p. 287.

7. Ibid.

8. Richard M. Cyert and James E. March, *A Behavioral Theory of the Firm* (Englewood Cliffs, N.J.: Prentice-Hall, 1964).

9. Schein, "Examining an Illusion," p. 290.

10. Ibid.

11. Ibid., p. 291.

12. Ibid., pp. 291–92.

13. Ibid., p. 292.

14. Peter Drucker, *Management: Tasks, Responsibilities and Practices* (New York: Harper & Row, 1974), p. 638.

15. Ibid., p. 639.

16. Ibid.

17. Ibid.

18. Ibid., p. 641.

19. William T. Greenwood, ed., *Management and Organizational Behavior Theories: An Interdisciplinary Approach* (Cincinnati, Ohio: South-Western, 1965), p. 45b. Subsequent material reprinted with permission.

20. Ibid.

21. Robert S. Weiss, "A Structure-Function Approach to Organization," *Journal of Social Issues* 12 (1956): 63. Reprinted with permission of *Social Issues* and author.

22. Ibid., p. 61.

23. Ibid.

24. Ibid., p. 66.

25. Greenwood, *Management and Organizational Behavior Theories*, p. 7.

26. Chris Argyris, "The Integration of the Individual and the Organization," in *Social Science Approaches to Business Behavior*, ed. George B. Strother (Homewood, Ill.: Dorsey Press, 1962), p. 58. Reprinted with permission.

27. Ibid., p. 61.

28. Ibid., p. 75.

29. Ibid., p. 79.

30. Fremont E. Kast, "Motivating the Organization Man," *Business Horizons*, Spring 1961, p. 58. Reprinted with permission of *Business Horizons*.

31. Ibid.

32. Ibid., p. 59.

33. Robert A. Dubin, "Person and Organization" (Paper presented at the 11th Annual Meeting—Industrial Research and the Discipline of Sociology—of the Industrial Relations Research Association, Madison, Wis., 1959), p. 161. Reprinted with permission of the Association.

34.   William Kornhauser, *Scientists in Industry* (Berkeley: University of California Press, 1962). Reprinted with permission.

35.   Ibid., p. 1.

36.   Alvin W. Gouldner, "Cosmopolitans and Locals: Toward an Analysis of Latent Social Roles, I," *Administrative Science Quarterly,* December 1957, pp. 281–306. Reprinted with permission.

37.   Ibid., p. 290.

38.   Loren Baritz, *The Servants of Power* (Middletown, Conn.: Wesleyan University Press, 1960).

39.   Ibid., p. 209.

40.   Ibid., p. 194.

41.   Matthew Radom, *The Social Scientist in American Industry* (New Brunswick, N.J.: Rutgers University Press, 1970).

42.   Abraham H. Maslow, *Motivation and Personality* (New York: Harper, 1954).

43.   Frederick Herzberg, *The Motivation to Work*, 2d ed. (New York: Wiley, 1959).

44.   David C. McClelland, *The Achieving Society* (Princeton, N.J.: Van Nostrand, 1961).

45.   Sigmund Freud, *Group Psychology and the Analysis of the Ego*, ed. John Strachey (New York: Norton, 1959), p. 6.

46.   Ibid., p. 61.

47.   Saul Scheidlinger, *Psychoanalysis and Group Behavior: A Study in Freudian Group Psychology* (New York: Norton, 1952), p. 89.

# PART II
# The Case Studied

# THE CASE STUDY APPROACH

To determine the way in which manifest and latent functions operate in the interaction between management consultants and their client organizations, the following questions will be broached through a case study approach:

1.  Why is the management consultant called in? What are the internal and external pressures bearing on the organization that result in the necessity of calling in the consultant? To what extent do these pressures shape management's definitions and presentations of the manifest presenting problems?
2.  To what extent are the manifest and latent problems explored by the consultant? What resistance to his exploration is encountered within the organization? What are the internal politics that affect the consultant?
3.  What is the impact of the management consultant on the organization? With reference to the presenting problems, what is the result of the consultant's intervention in terms of the manifest and latent functions? To what extent are changes implemented and to what extent are the consultant's recommendations influenced by the organization's politics?

The gathering of data and the analysis of the case study will be based on the following model.

The background on the organization section includes the history and development of the organization that is examined in the case study. It details the structure and nature of the company and the utilities industry. Its location and size are given as well as significant events that occurred over a ten-year period.

The presenting problems, as given by company management to the consultant at the time of entry into the organization, are described, along with the consultant's specific assignment. The manifest and latent functions that serve to form and define the presenting problems will be discussed in this context. Once the assignment is undertaken, the role of social structure and latent functions in confirming, redefining, and implementing solutions to the presenting problems will also be the object of investigation. This will include the social and political pressures bearing on problem definition and redefinition; and the processes of co-optation, conflict, and compromise involved in problem resolution will be explored. The process of diagnosis will be seen as a continuously moving response to presenting problems, theory, manifest experience and objective realities, and latent structural pressures.

The response of the organization as a whole to the solutions of presenting problems and subsequent ones as presented by the consulting firm will be assessed. This section will include a discussion of the way the solutions are accepted or rejected and any conflict that might be engendered by them. There will also be a discussion of the new problems that appear to be caused by conflict arising through acceptance of the findings of the consultant and by the implementation of the findings themselves.

The case study method will be used to explore the politics of management consulting in a particular organization. The case study will present in detail—following the outline of the proposed model—an examination of how several consultants functioned in this organization. The extent to which similar processes are present and whether each consultant functions in unique ways will be noted in the final chapter.

In concluding, the study will present the basis for a theory of *politics of management consulting* as well as a theory of the relationship between manifest theory and practice in the ambiguous jungle of the business organization.

The study will also suggest how latent functions and motivations affect the application of theory and science in complex social structures and how objective social reality is always modified by subjective factors.

Field data were drawn from the observations and diaries of the author as he worked within the organization as a management trainer, internal consultant, and adviser to executive personnel. These observations will be presented in the course of the case study and the discussion describing in specifics how management consultants operated in the organization with respect to techniques or processes and manifest and latent functions.

Background data were derived from newspapers, journals, government publications, reports of consultant firms, and reports of the organization itself. These sources include the Hearings of the Equal Employment Opportunity Commission, the Bureau of Labor Statistics, and reports of major consultant firms. The data provide background on the company and the external and internal pressures bearing on organizations that have affected their use of management consultants.

Additional data have been provided by books and journal articles, which provide current research and theoretical background on management consulting, social science theories, and organizational behavior. There is only a small amount of literature written about management consulting that pertains to this case study. The literature cited here represents the current body of sources.

Part II will focus on a case study of a utility from 1967 to 1977 as it employed several management consultants to help manage its complex problems. Chapter 3 provides a description of the client organization in terms of the utilities industry and background on events and pressures that led to the hiring of five management consultants during a two-year period. Chapter 4 describes how each consultant was hired, the problems presented to them, the way they entered the company, and the style and approach the consultants used to handle their assignments. Outcomes of consultancy will be explained in terms of the manifest and latent effects on the company and in terms of the impact of social science theories the consultants utilized.

In the case study that will be examined, there are three areas of emphasis that the organization recognized as problems and decided to remedy. These areas will be presented as separate problems for the purpose of analysis, but—in the main— undoubtedly the inability of responsible management to resolve problems and make decisions gave rise to the three presenting problems that will be addressed.

These problems are *management style, race relations,* and *finance.* They are interrelated in that they all involve the overall management of the company and reflect not only organizational policy but management practice as well.

Deficient management practices may result in a lack of long-range planning and poor decision making, both of which can lead to or aggravate financial difficulties. In addition, some of the financial problems the company faced were created by influences often beyond the company's control. For example, changes in accounting procedures required the approval of the Public Service Commission (PSC), and changes in taxation required passage of special laws by the state legislature. State regulations regarding the precise procedures for the company's borrowing money and floating bonds were quite costly and not to the company's advantage. Other external constraints came from the state Power Pool regulations on the purchase and transmission of power, federal safety laws, EEO laws, and the PSC. These had a strong influence on the way the company was run and on its inherently high costs in relation to other utilities.

Although the financial aspect of the company was a problem, it will not be treated in the same depth of analysis as the company's other problems. Since the focus of the case study will be on the relationship between the consultant and the client, the financial aspect will not be directly addressed because the author was not exposed to financial discussions and the policy issues of the firm. Furthermore, it is the social science consultants who will be the primary object of analysis rather than the technical consultants. The fixed procedures and budgetary constraints under which a utility operates force the company into standard financial practices.

# THREE

# The Client Organization

## DESCRIPTION OF THE CLIENT COMPANY

The organization that will be examined in this case study is a privately owned East Coast utility that provides gas, steam, and electricity. It is not only one of the oldest dispensers of energy but also one of the largest in the country. It is the biggest utility in the nation in terms of numbers of electricity customers. It serves 8.9 million residents within an area of 660 square miles. It has an installed capacity of 8.6 million kilowatts. It is the largest privately owned gas-electricity utility in the United States. If it were classified as a corporation, it would rank in the top 50 of the Fortune 500.

This utility is the city's biggest real estate taxpayer, paying 8 percent of the city's real estate taxes.[1] The company has about 22,700 employees of whom 4,800 are management and 17,900 are hourly employees. The hourly employees are members of one of two labor unions: a few hundred belong to the International Brotherhood of Electrical Workers and the rest belong to a local of the Utility Workers of America. Some background and history of the company will provide a general picture of its position in the utilities industry.

This company was founded in 1823 as one of the first gas companies in the country. Its electric operations go back to 1882 when it became one of the first electric utilities in the nation. It began supplying electricity for 400 lamps in offices in the city from Thomas A. Edison's original generating station.[2] The present name was adopted in 1936 after a series of mergers involving a number of small gas and electric companies in the metropolitan area. A steam company was merged in 1954, putting the company in the business of supplying steam to most of the large buildings in the city.[3]

The state affects the company through its general economic climate. For example, the amount of unemployment in the state, manpower availability, general economic trends affecting business, and any state policies toward the city all have consequences for the utility. Some of the state laws that affect the utility in its daily operations are state labor laws, state equal employment opportunity regulations, and environmental and safety laws. Many of these areas also have city and federal requirements, too. State laws affecting interest rates or regulating banks also affect the company in relation to its loans and the purchase or sale of its bonds.

The state is one of several agencies that have a great impact on the company because of its direct involvement through the PSC. To help better understand the financial condition of the company from 1967 to 1977, it will be necessary to explore the influence of state policies and the PSC.

The PSC was created by the state legislature. It is composed of a chairman, who is selected by the governor, and five commissioners, who are appointed by the governor with the consent of the state senate for six-year terms. Only as recently as 1974 was legislation passed making the PSC bipartisan. Under the law no more than three of its five commissioners may be members of the same political party.[4]

The PSC regulates public utilities operating in the state. There are some areas in which its authority is superseded by the Federal Power Commission, but they are few in number. It has jurisdiction over rates, service, and long-range planning of all electric, gas, steam, telephone and telegraph, and waterworks companies. It also licenses sites for electric and gas transmission lines placement. In 1972 a special State Board on Electric Generation Siting and the Environment was created by the legislature to provide one-step certification of environmental compatibility and public need for major steam-electric generation plants.[5]

The PSC conducts investigations, holds public hearings, and decides hundreds of cases each year. Federal regulation by the Federal Power Commission (FPC) is required for nuclear plants.

The PSC is given six major functions:

1. Determination of reasonable rates to be charged consumers.

2. Supervision of operations of utilities to assure safe, adequate and reliable operation and service.

3. Supervision and control over financing.

4. Certification of public need and environmental suitability of routes of construction, and operating plans for proposed electrical and gas transmission lines.

5. Participation in administration of power plant legislation (in conjunction with the special Board above).

6. Promotion of long-term planning by utilities with concern for public safety, environment and conservation of natural resources.[6]

## NATURE OF THE ORGANIZATION

The company has a **hierarchical structure** typical of U.S. business. Prior to 1969 the company was organized into department by function. When the new chairman took office in 1967, there were a total of 23 executives in the organization. There were 12 departments, each with a vice-president reporting directly to the president (who, in turn, reported to the chairman). By 1977 the number of executives had increased to 37. In 1969 a major change occurred as the organization became decentralized: 6 operating departments and 5 other departments were created, bringing the total number to 23 departments. The 6 operating departments were divided according to geographical location. This decentralization epitomized what **Peter Drucker** referred to when he wrote about big business being a confederation of smaller businesses, each with its own strategy.[7]

The organization thereby became similar to what **William Greenwood** describes as *functionalized staff*. It had geographically decentralized units and centralized control through the top levels of the hierarchy, which provided policies.[8]

Another level of management was created at the same time by appointing five executive vice-presidents responsible for major areas of the company and having them report directly to the chairman. All department and division vice-presidents then reported to an executive vice-president. This imposition of a new level in the hierarchy made the structure even more like a pyramid and closer to the military structure. This also constituted another step in the chain of command and reduced the authority of the vice-presidents, who were once decision makers and administrators, to only being administrators.

In the same year the offices of the president and chairman were combined. A combined office existed until 1973 when the president became vice-chairman and a new president was appointed. The president's position regained its autonomy, and the executive vice-presidents again reported to the president.

In 1975 the vice-chairman and the president retired, and another new president was appointed with the additional title of chief operating officer (CEO). While maintaining direct supervision of the operating divisions, the new president appointed two assistant vice-presidents with staff functions. When one assistant vice-president left the organization, a senior vice-president of operations was moved up to the staff position and relinquished his line responsibility.

Other changes in the organization during this time that are of interest are the expansion in 1969 of the general auditor's office to include the mandate for examining the company's operations and recommending improvements; the establishment of a Department of Environmental Affairs in 1970, which was combined in 1974 with the Construction and Engineering Departments; and the increase in the Employee Relations Department from 12 employees in 1970 to 77 employees in 1975. During 1975 the company also hired over 500 new employees to work in the Customer Service Department in an attempt to improve efficiency and restore its image through an intensive public relations campaign.

It is also worthy of mention that as late as 1968, the company's data processing system was outmoded. Because of this, management was not provided with the information it needed for coordination and long-term planning.

The utility was typical of its industry in its occupational structure. The steam, gas, and electric industries are basically made up of (1) construction and installation of electrical services by underground cables or overhead wires and maintenance of these services; (2) power generation (steam, electricity); and (3) distribution of gas, electricity, and steam.

Most jobs fall into the two broad categories of *power plant operations*, and *transmission and distribution*. In addition, there are clerical, professional, and customer service positions.

Jobs in power plant operations involve observation, control, and record-keeping functions of power generation equipment as well as maintenance and repair functions. There are boiler, turbine, auxiliary equipment, and switch operators. In plants where these operations have been centralized or automated, control room operators perform these duties.

In the transmission and distribution areas, jobs are for load dispatchers, substation operators, linemen and troublemen, and gas main fitters.

The industry provides opportunities for *on-the-job training* and *advancement* in its craft positions. Entry into craft jobs is not as difficult in the utilities as it is in other industries, and its craftsmen are highly paid in comparison with those in many other industries. Generally, most positions are filled from within the company. The uniqueness of the skills required and the heavy dependence on in-house training mean that relatively few workers are able to transfer skills acquired in the company to other industries for comparable salaries.

Historically, the utilities industry has had a low turnover rate and a reliance on employee referrals for recruiting new personnel. With the bulk of employees coming from Irish and Italian backgrounds, their referrals were from the same ethnic groups. At the time of the founding of the industry, most utilities were located in the North and the West. Since almost 90 percent of the country's blacks lived in the South at that time, there was very little employment of blacks by utilities. Until the loss of farm occupations caused a large migration of blacks to northern urban areas in the 1950s and 1960s, these patterns had not changed appreciably.

Once the utility had created its basic technology, further increases in the demand for electricity could be met without an increase in the number of employees, owing to the growth of automatic controls and other types of mechanization. Although overall work could still provide ample employment, restrictions on maintenance and capital expenditures during the 1970s caused a job freeze in the company and a transfer of excess personnel to other departments where it was possible.

The job freeze was exacerbated by the sale of two nuclear generating stations to the state Power Authority in 1975, and the cost of producing power with old equipment led the company to cut back on its generation of power. They relied more and more on the purchase of power from elsewhere to be transmitted and distributed by the company to its customers.

In the clerical and office work areas, increased electronic data processing and computerized billing and record keeping led to little or no new employment.

This utility can be classified as a high-slack organization. High-slack organizations or systems, as previously noted, are those operating within a reasonably stable environment requiring rather routine functioning and the maintenance of day-to-day activities to continue to operate in an effective manner.[9] Many of the jobs in the company are repetitive and routine. Even jobs that have higher educational requirements (such as engineers) actually demand little more than pushing buttons or watching dials. The company is known for its excessive personnel and duplication of effort at the management level. With increased automation the company was now capable of delivering the same kilowatt power with fewer people. This contributed to the high slack in the company because there were more people producing the same or less.

The nature of the organization as a high-slack system was demonstrated when the bargaining unit went out on strike in 1968. Management, with the work force reduced to a third, was still able to maintain services. The outcome was what many had predicted—increased efficiency by trimming the fat or "deadwood."

It is also necessary to understand the nature of the company in terms of its management climate. This utility had a hierarchical structure that had both centralized and decentralized authority with power concentrated in the CEO—the chairman—and simultaneously decentralized into five divisions, each with its own vice-president. The military background of the chairman reinforced the hierarchical structure.

As **Robert Jackall** describes it, the key to the structure is the reporting system. This forms a feudal-like system of norms wherein each "subordinate owes a fealty to his immediate boss: he must not overcommit his boss; he must keep his boss from mistakes, especially public ones; he must not circumvent his boss."[10] It is characteristic of this "feudal-like authority system that details are pushed down and credit is pushed up."[11] There are also negative sanctions for public criticism.

The great influence that the CEO has in his own company should also be noted. Jackall draws the analogy to a king: "His word is law; even his wishes and whims are taken as commands by his close subordinates. . . ."[12] In this utility every effort is, indeed, made to please the chairman. One example of this is the high priority and money that was allocated to housekeeping (cleanliness of the plant) because the chairman liked things to be neat. Another example was the 15-hour days that many plant managers spent, not necessarily working but just being there because they felt it would not "look good" in case the chairman happened to come to their plant and they were not there (the chairman was known for making surprise visits at odd hours).

## BACKGROUND LEADING TO THE USE OF OUTSIDE CONSULTANTS

Five years after World War II, the utility was in an expansionist phase. It was still merging with other small companies in the area—two companies in 1951, one in 1952, and a steam company in 1954. In 1956 the company allocated $650 million for a five-year expansion plan; in 1959 they planned $1 billion for a five-year expansion program, with over 90 percent to be used for electric generating and distributing.[13] Electric rates were being reduced in areas where natural gas was being used.[14] By approving the mergers, the PSC was also helping the company to avoid intervention by the Federal Power Commission (FPC). The FPC claimed jurisdiction because the parent company had planned to resell natural gas obtained through interstate commerce. The PSC had disapproved the same merger in 1945 because at that time the company had planned to raise the city's rates to make them the same as the county's. In 1959 the company purchased three power plants from the city subway system.[15]

During this period, new facilities were being planned or built; in particular, a new generating station was begun in one of the divisions.

The company's bond rating and rates are critical since they are the principal means of raising capital for the company. In the 1950s their bond rating was good and interest rates were low (around 5 percent). Credit was also good: in 1955, 15 banks granted loans of $100 million.[16] Again in 1958 they were granted $100 million in credit for one year.[17] The PSC authorized selling $75 million worth of 30-year refunding mortgage bonds; they sold in December of 1959 at 5.19 percent.[18]

The 1960s began the first hints of problems to follow with the start of the chain of increases in electric rates granted by the PSC. In January of 1960 a $14 million annual increase was approved by the state for electricity rates in spite of opposition from other agencies.[19] The PSC refused requests for a rehearing on rates by the mayor, allowing the company to make interim boosts in electricity rates.[20]

In 1961 the PSC awarded a rate increase of $10.5 million while suggesting that the company increase its rates for large users (cities and railroads) and lower costs slightly to small users.[21] In 1963 the PSC was challenged in the state appeals court for the rate increase in electricity it had granted the year before; the court upheld the increase.[22] Later, however, the PSC told the company to postpone its scheduled increase of 5 percent in electric rates.[23] It also conducted an investigation to determine if the firm was charging too much for gas.[24] As a result of its investigation, the PSC ordered the company to reduce gas rates by $6.5 million annually.[25]

Six months later the company was allowed a 5 percent hike in electric rates. In state court the court of appeals heard a suit brought by the City Housing Authority to protest the 5 percent increase granted by the PSC. In their suit the housing authority claimed that customers were being charged for the purchase of the three subway power stations that had been purchased in 1959. They claimed that the company had paid a high price solely to eliminate city competition. The appellate division found no evidence of overpayment and refused to overturn the increase.[26]

The increase continued to be fought in court, and in 1966 the state court of appeals ordered the PSC to reconsider the rate increase.[27]

In July of the same year (1966), the company once again asked the PSC for a rise in rates because of higher taxes and inflation.[28] When this met with strong opposition from the community, the company agreed to postpone the increase for 60 days. Promptly two months later they were permitted to raise electric and steam rates, although they cut gas rates by 4 percent.[29] (At that time natural gas was plentiful and inexpensive; therefore, it was being promoted for consumer use by reducing the rates.)

By 1967 the company was experiencing difficulties in several areas. A former undersecretary to a cabinet position was brought in as chairman to help change the company's image and, with his political influence, to help promote the construction of nuclear power plants, which had been encountering opposition at the local level. A headline in the *Wall Street Journal* at that time was: "Unhappy Utility: Bad Image, Inefficiency, Bloated Work Force Halt Firm's Progress; New Chairman Retires Aging Executives, Trims Costs, Defends High Power Rates."[30]

The new chairman took over the problems of poor public relations, an aging physical plant, and mounting financial difficulties. The chairman, coming from a military background, placed others from military backgrounds in key administrative positions as he tried to get the company to become more "efficient."

The most dramatic problem of the 1960s involved the citywide blackout in 1965. After that failure concern mounted over future power needs. In 1969, shortly after the PSC began an investigation of why the company's largest plant was out of service, the company asked for a 15.3 percent increase in electric rates,[31] claiming it had the lowest return (3.77 percent) of all major utilities (7.0 percent).[32] They also claimed that inflation; taxes; cost of wages, equipment, and supplies; environmental costs; and higher interest rates necessitated a large increase. The PSC, in response to the request, temporarily stopped the increase and eventually approved only part of it, citing the company's failure to take advantage of Internal Revenue Service (IRS) depreciation guidelines and its failure to provide adequate service.[33] The PSC predicted possible shortages in the company's electric power supply by 1970.[34]

By the 1970s it was apparent to everyone and openly admitted that the company was in serious trouble. In July of 1970 the firm's stock closed at the lowest point it had reached since 1949.[35] The company's requests for rate increases became more frequent. In 1970 they were granted an increase of $90 million in electric rates by the PSC. This was less than they had requested. In granting the increase a PSC member blamed conservationists, in part, for the utility's financial need.[36]

The 1970s began a more active and influential role by conservationists and was accompanied by more restrictions because of environmental regulations. These were often quite costly. Pollution charges became more frequent and were enforced more stringently.[37]

For the first time in 12 years, the company asked for an increase in gas rates.[38] Steam rates went up with the permission of the PSC.[39]

Although there were shortages of power in the city, blackouts or outages were averted by the purchase of power from other sources: Canada, the Atomic Energy Commission (AEC), and other utilities on the East Coast. The company joined with other utilities in the state to form a power pool. According to the New York *Times* of September 7, 1970, for "all practical purposes the entire state has a single power system that is coordinated from . . . Power Pool Headquarters. . . ."[40] At the same time, the company was being criticized for lack of planning of transmission line routes because they now had to turn down power offers for lack of transmission lines.[41] Although the company received increases in electric rates, they did not receive as much as they had requested.[42]

The year 1971 marked the start of a new advertising campaign. For the first time the company was asking customers to use **less** electricity.[43] This was necessary because of their lack of generating capacity and because of their pollution problems.

With the oil crisis of 1973 problems for the company multiplied. In addition to higher fuel prices, their credit rating was lowered by major rating agencies[44] so that they had difficulty selling their bonds. Several rate increases were granted by the PSC, and permission was given to burn higher-sulfur oil temporarily. In spite of this the company was unable to maintain a good financial position.

Public relations was at a low. The PSC asserted that they were unresponsive to customer complaints (handling only 46 percent adequately).[45] Uncollectible unpaid accounts receivable became a greater problem. From 1967 to 1973 uncollected bills over six months old rose from $2.2 million to $34.4 million. To reduce this amount, the company expanded their accounting department and requested that the PSC allow them to charge interest on unpaid bills in the same way that retail stores do.[46] The company claimed that the reasons for uncollected bills were "the large number of underprivileged and welfare customers as well as the poor bill-paying habits of many of its customers, and resentment over sharp rate increases."[47] Others pointed out that the poor billing practices of the company and the large errors it made in bills also contributed to this dilemma.

At the end of 1973 the company was told by the state PSC to cut voltage by 3 percent to save fuel.[48] At the same time they were pleading for the PSC to quickly approve a rate increase of $296.6 million yearly because of their "desperate" need.[49]

Although the PSC granted an immediate rate hike in February of 1974, a serious cash squeeze led to a suspension of the company's quarterly dividend for the first time in their history.[50] According to state and regulatory officials, Wall Street analysts, and former company employees, the company had some of the most serious financial and operating difficulties of any utility in the country. Internal operating and management problems, environmental concerns and energy shortages, inflation and high interest rates, a downturn in new business, and customer problems all combined to precipitate the situation. The company had nearly reached its growth limit in terms of customers in its market.

With increasing capital needs to replace old and inefficient power units as well as to finance current operations, there were alternatives: either raise rates or increase the amount of electricity consumed. Conservation requirements precluded the latter. The difficulty in selling bonds (with the highest rate in the country of 9.48), low rating by bond-rating agencies, and lack of investor confidence all contributed to the capital shortage.[51]

In addition, only through a change in accounting procedures by the PSC in December 1973 for all the state's utilities was the company able to have enough "net earnings available for interest legally to be allowed to issue its bonds. The state agency [PSC] permitted the utility to carry forward on its books the amount paid for its fuel until it could bill its customers for the money."[52]

On the other hand, the PSC required the company to use a method of financing that the company claimed was too costly. Under this arrearage financing, the utility borrows on short term from banks until it reaches its limits on short-term credit and then floats long-term bonds to pay back the banks. With high interest rates and the credit squeeze, this costs the company a great deal of money.[53]

If the company cannot produce enough revenue, the New York *Times* projected that the consequences would necessitate either "substantial tax abatements on state and city real estate tax or even outright government takeover of all or part of its operations."[54]

Some critics felt that the suspension of dividends was a tactic dictated by politics as well as economics. The company was willing to penalize its stockholders, according to the *Economist*, "to help persuade city and state that it must be helped."[55] The company was asking not only for a rate increase but also for the "state to purchase two unfinished nuclear power plants, on which it has spent $450 million, and to sell [the company] back the power. Unless the state provides such assistance, [the company] may eventually face bankruptcy."[56]

**George Cabot Lodge**, a professor at Harvard Business School and a recognized expert on this utility, proposed that since the company's difficulties were so vast, it should be broken up by dividing it in half: the production, generating plants, and new construction would be taken over by the state, while distribution and marketing would be retained by the company. Another proposal was that the company cut its dividend on common stock and obtain government subsidies either through tax abatements or through state-guaranteed bonds up to the point of a tax exemption.[57] All solutions proposed involved the state in some way.

The company itself requested help from the state. Declaring that they faced bankruptcy,[58] they urged the state to buy their two unfinished nuclear plants. This required the passage of a special bill by the state legislature. Under this plan the State Power Authority would buy and complete the nuclear generating plants.[59] While awaiting the proceeds from the sale, the PSC authorized an increase of bank loans to $425 million to provide additional cash.[60]

It is interesting to note that while the company was pleading for the state to take over its plants in 1974, the company had vehemently opposed any active government role in 1967. At that time there had been a suggested proposition to the state constitution elaborating a state policy on public power. The proposition read: "The development and expansion of public power in the state is a matter of important concern to the economic growth of the state and general welfare of the people, and provisions for such development and expansion shall be made by the state in such a manner and by such means as the legislature shall from time to time determine."[61] At a hearing held on the state's role in the development of power, spokesmen for the company and the six other investor-owned utilities in the state told the committee, "There is no further need whatever for further development and expansion of tax-exempt public power in the state."[62] Seven years later, the company reversed its policy by asking the state to take over its two nuclear generating plants.

An additional external pressure bearing down on the company came from the federal government. The utility was asked to testify before the U.S. *Equal Employment Opportunity Commission (EEOC)*. The EEOC held special hearings on the utilization of minority and women workers in the public utilities industry on November 15, 1971, in Washington, D.C. At these hearings it was stated that the utilities lagged behind other major employers in the country in terms of their employment of minorities and women, both in the quality of jobs held and in numbers. In fact, the electrical power industry had the worst record of all industries.

In testifying at the hearings, the utility's assistant vice-president (AVP) of employee relations tried to show the company's good faith in its affirmative action efforts. The AVP testified: "It is our objective to have all levels of management take aggressive measures to make our affirmative action program a living document producing greater employment and promotion opportunities for minority groups and women."[63]

These series of events—lasting over a number of years and being much publicized—made it necessary for the company to employ a wide variety of management consultants. For example, it was obligated to bring in consultants to validate the AVP's testimony at the EEOC.

The late 1960s evidenced the stress and strain within this utility, which intensified over a ten-year period. It began in 1967 when the new chairman was appointed. His first official function was to retire some older executives in an attempt to make the organization more efficient. Ten years later, the company was still trying to rid itself of excessive personnel. A chronology of events suggests some of the utility's problems and its attempts to cope with them.

## CHRONOLOGY OF EVENTS, 1967–77

1967   A former government official is made chairman. He retires "aging" executives and tries to trim costs.

1968   The bargaining unit goes out on strike. This is the first time in the history of the company that its management personnel assume all of the functions necessary to continue the utility's services.

1970   The company's stock closes at the lowest point in over two decades.
       The JOBS '70 (Job Opportunities in the Business Sector) program begins.

1971   The company receives its first opinion and attitude survey of its management employees by hiring consultant OAS.
       The company testifies at the EEOC hearings.

1973   The company hires the first minority in a middle-management staff position with responsibility for diagnosing and suggesting solutions to organizational problems.
       The company's management training programs begin.

1974   The company suspends its stock dividend for the first time in its history.
       Consultant FLO is hired to develop selection and hiring criteria that would be nondiscriminatory and valid for job performance.

1975   Consultant BCF is hired by the PSC to conduct a study of management operations.

A study is conducted by the author: "Job Satisfaction of Black and White Managers."

The State Education Department, Office of Non-Collegiate Sponsored Instruction, recommends that college credits be awarded to personnel completing company management training programs.

1976     Consultant ABC is hired to conduct leadership-style workshops for middle managers.

Consultant CRY is hired to develop a Planning and Scheduling System.

Consultant BPA is hired to help implement the CRY system as an organizational development effort.

The AVP makes a statement about blacks, which causes racial antagonism in the company.

The CEO is virtually held captive in his office by a group of minority employees.

An EEO suit is filed against the company by an internal consultant.

1977     Some 211 management employees are fired.

An EEO suit is filed by some of the fired managers, charging the company with age discrimination.

The AVP is scapegoated and dismissed.

As evidenced by the chronology, this giant organization was faced for over a decade with a myriad of different problems and situations that had a tremendous impact on the organization. The problems and conflicts that arose over new demands, resistance to change, and the insistence that social equality be demonstrated in the work world all caused the organization to focus more on the hiring of social scientists as consultants to work on different organizational issues created by these pressures.

For the purpose of this study, five detailed analyses will be made of the use of management consultants by the company. In each case the consultant's entry into the organization, the problems as presented to the consultant, the consultant's approach and style, and the outcomes of the consultancy will be described.

The problems of the most sensitive nature, which involved consultants with a human relations background, were issues that included managers' motivation, self-identity, and styles of leadership. These rather than the other stated problems (such as poor communication, no differential between pay of supervisors and union workers, and shift scheduling) were seen by the company as critical to the improvement of the organization.


## THE JOBS '70S PROGRAM

Problems engendered by the attitudes of the white male employees toward minorities and women in the company were given the lowest priority. The statement made by union and supervisory personnel that illustrated this feeling was: "The electricity will still be produced and distributed—whether or not the company has women and minorities."

This matter of racial and sex bias came to light during the hiring and placement of minorities and women within the company through the JOBS '70s program. The JOBS program was a special program begun as a response to external pressures to hire minorities and women in business. However, many first-line supervisors and middle managers felt that newly hired minority employees were undermining the company and the integrity of the system since they felt the new personnel did not have the basic qualifications for the jobs. Racial and sex prejudices were aggravated because the JOBS applicants were recruited in a non-traditional fashion.

As a federally supported project, the JOBS program recruited its applicants from the State Employment Service, the Manpower Career Agency, and the state Central Labor Council. As stated before, previous new employees had been referrals from personnel already in the company. Thus it was not unusual to have three generations of a family working in the company at one time. Employing husband and wife or father and son was common practice. It should be noted that at the same time the author functioned as a staff trainer and internal consultant, his son was a worker in the bargaining unit. Some of the author's neighbors were also members of the company, all working at the same location.

The applicants in the JOBS program had to be certified as "disadvantaged." The connotations and stereotypes associated with this term also fed into the prejudices of existing employees.

There were a variety of skill levels brought in through this program—some workers were unskilled and uneducated (less than sixth grade), while others ran the gamut from high school dropouts, to high school graduates, to some who had completed one or two years of college.

The JOBS program provided a two-day intake process for job applicants in which descriptions and the realities of entry-level jobs were discussed. These jobs, production personnel and general utility mechanic (GUM), were two positions for which the JOBS '70s program trained people. These positions clearly required very little formal education, but they were unskilled jobs that led to higher-skilled and higher-paid craft positions.

After the intake process, the program provided 13 weeks of basic education. The program included English as a second language, verbal and arithmetic skills, and vestibule training (a simulation of field conditions in the classroom).

The next phase of the program was 26 weeks of on-the-job training for perfecting skills. The training included basic electricity, gas operations, pipe fitting, rigging, cable pulling, power plant operations, pipe tapping, splicing, excavating, job safety, job setup, equipment maintenance, and repair of power plants. This was the first time that skills training had been centralized and taken out of the field. Prior to the JOBS program, training had always been done in the field with a more experienced employee demonstrating how to perform the job for which the unskilled employee had been hired.

In testifying before the EEOC hearings in 1971, the AVP of employee relations explained that the training provided for the minorities entering through the JOBS '70s program was aimed at what the trainee would need to perform the job. Training was not needed to qualify the minorities for the job (since they were unskilled positions) but to "provide our field forces with an employee *better* [emphasis added] qualified than those we employ through our normal employment procedures."[64] The company claimed that this was done specifically to enhance the acceptance of minorities by their supervisors. Supervisors, on the other hand, perceived the situation as just the opposite. To them the minorities were "less qualified" because they had not come in the "normal" way.

## NOTES

1.  New York *Times*, March 31, 1974, p. 1.
2.  Ibid.
3.  *Moody's Public Utilities Manual* (New York: Moody's Investor Service, 1975), p. 189.
4.  *New York Red Book* (Albany, N.Y.: Williams Press, 1975), p. 849.
5.  Ibid.
6.  Ibid.
7.  Peter Drucker, *Management: Tasks, Responsibilities, Practices* (New York: Harper & Row, 1974), p. 641.
8.  William T. Greenwood, ed., *Management and Organizational Behavior Theories: An Interdisciplinary Approach* (Cincinnati, Ohio: South-Western, 1965), p. 456.
9.  Virginia Schein, "Examining an Illusion: The Role of Deceptive Behaviors in Organizations," *Human Relations* 32 (1979): 290.
10.  Copyright © (1983) by the President and Fellows of Harvard College; all rights reserved. Reprinted by permission of the *Harvard Business Review.* "Moral Mazes: Bureaucracy and Managerial Work" by Robert Jackall, (In press).
11.  Ibid.
12.  Ibid.
13.  *Wall Street Journal*, March 25, 1959, p. 14.
14.  New York *Times*, February 16, 1951, p. 27.
15.  *Wall Street Journal*, May 20, 1959, p. 2.
16.  New York *Times*, October 5, 1955, p. 47.
17.  Ibid., September 27, 1958, p. 27.
18.  *Wall Street Journal*, December 2, 1959, p. 19.
19.  Ibid., January 14, 1960, p. 14.
20.  Ibid., February 9, 1960, p. 3.
21.  Ibid., November 17, 1961, p. 8.
22.  Ibid., February 12, 1963, p. 5.
23.  Ibid., September 26, 1963, p. 20.
24.  Ibid., December 12, 1963, p. 8.
25.  Ibid., January 23, 1964, p. 4.
26.  New York *Times*, November 28, 1965, p. 72.
27.  *Wall Street Journal*, April 29, 1966, p. 8.
28.  Ibid., July 29, 1966, p. 8.
29.  Ibid., November 23, 1966, p. 10.
30.  Ibid., August 26, 1968, p. 1.
31.  Ibid., August 22, 1969, p. 15.
32.  New York *Times*, September 7, 1970, p. 18.
33.  Ibid.

34.  *Wall Street Journal*, December 4, 1969, p. 16.

35.  New York *Times*, July 30, 1970, p. 22.

36.  *Wall Street Journal*, June 18, 1970, p. 18.

37.  Ibid., October 14, 1970, p. 3.

38.  Ibid., September 21, 1970, p. 20.

39.  Ibid., December 18, 1970, p. 10.

40.  Ibid.

41.  New York *Times*, September 7, 1970, p. 18.

42.  *Wall Street Journal*, November 29, 1971, p. 10.

43.  Ibid., May 4, 1971, p. 17.

44.  Ibid., February 1, 1973, p. 23

45.  Ibid., February 28, 1973, p. 19.

46.  New York *Times*, April 1, 1974, p. 51.

47.  Ibid.

48.  *Wall Street Journal*, December 26, 1973, p. 10.

49.  Ibid., December 31, 1973, p. 6.

50.  New York *Times*, April 24, 1974, p. 1.

51.  Ibid., March 31, 1974, p. 46.

52.  Ibid.

53.  Ibid., April 1, 1974, p. 51.

54.  Ibid., March 31, 1974, p. 46.

55.  *Economist*, April 27, 1974, p. 251.

56.  *Wall Street Journal*, April 27, 1974, p. 65.

57.  New York *Times*, April 1, 1974, p. 51.

58.  Ibid., May 10, 1974, p. 1.

59.  *Wall Street Journal*, May 17, 1974, p. 5.

60.  Ibid., September 12, 1974, p. 27.

61.  "A State's Role in the Development of Power," *Public Utilities Fortnightly*, August 3, 1967, p. 53.

62.  Ibid.

63.  U.S., Equal Employment Opportunity Commission, *Hearings before the United States Equal Employment Opportunity Commission on Utilization of Minority and Women Workers in the Public Utilities Industry* (Washington, D.C.: EEOC, November 15, 1971), p. 16.

64.  Ibid., p. 18.

# F O U R

# Consultant Cases

## CONSULTANT OAS

The first consultant during this period to enter the organization was a consulting firm from the midwestern United States—**OAS**. As specialists in attitude surveys they were well known for their research on employee motivation. In 1971 they were brought into the company at the request of top management. Their assignment was to conduct a *survey* on the *opinions and attitudes of management* employees to find out whether the managers were dissatisfied with any areas in the company.

A vice-president requested the survey because some lower-level managers were talking about forming a supervisory union, even though it was illegal for managers to belong to a bargaining unit. Although these managers were small in number, the prospect of unionization of supervisors was a serious threat. The survey represented a way for top management to indicate concern about managers' feelings and attitudes without losing control of the situation.

The attitude survey form was jointly developed by the company management and the professional staff of OAS. It was administered—in person by OAS staff members—to management employees of the company in 1971 on April 27, 28, 29, and 30. A total of 3,991 managers of all levels at various locations in the company received the survey form. The survey form consisted of sets of statements to which degrees of satisfaction/dissatisfaction or agreement/disagreement were shown by a check mark. The statements referred to a number of aspects of one's job—for example, working conditions, benefits, wages, communication, supervision, and management. These aspects were designed to "bring to light areas of dissatisfaction and discontent."[1]

Of the five levels of management represented in the survey (3,991), the two reports of OAS covering first- and second-level managers and the survey of middle managers will be explained here in detail and referred to again later. On each table the weighted average for each item as well as the number of favorable and unfavorable written comments was given. For the first- and second-level supervisors (N = 2,171), there were 10,100 comments (an average of 4.7 per person, according to OAS). For middle managers (N = 664), there were 3,918 comments (an average of 5.9 per person, according to OAS).

It should be noted that the comments and results presented here are those of OAS. It is difficult to draw sound conclusions from their work since there was not enough information given by OAS.

A total of 2,171 first- and second-level supervisors completed the survey. OAS reported that overall the first- and second-level **supervisors** were pleased with most aspects of the company. According to the OAS summary comments, the company benefits (such as vacation, holidays, life insurance, sick pay plan) and most aspects of their working conditions were also acceptable to them.

Attitudes toward immediate supervision were generally positive. Top management was viewed as being concerned with problems of pollution, committed to the preservation of the environment, and responsive to the social and economic needs of the community. Most of the supervisors were proud of their association with the company and, with some reservations, would recommend the company to their friends as a good place to work. There was strong approval of annual performance reviews, and they strongly supported the idea that promotions should be made primarily on merit and not on the basis of seniority.

The OAS report related some dissatisfaction registered toward various aspects of the job, that is, receiving direction from more than one boss, having their superiors bypass them by going directly to their subordinates, changing priorities constantly, working too much overtime, doing too much paperwork, being allowed too little time for planning, and getting too much pressure to produce. Disfavor was expressed toward the degree to which they were consulted before decisions were made concerning their area of responsibility—for example, on hiring or transfers of personnel, on promotions, on dismissals, and on new policies and procedures.

*Supervisors* were unhappy with the advice and guidance they received from upper management, explanations on how to deal with the union, and backing from higher management on handling disciplinary problems. They were also somewhat dissatisfied with the specific help they received from middle management toward meeting their departmental goals and objectives. They would have liked to be better informed regarding anticipated changes that may have affected their work or that of their subordinates. Similarly, they would have liked more attention given to their recommendations on hiring and firing.

Several other areas of dissatisfaction dealt with aspects of their pay—the differential between their annual pay and that of those reporting to them was small or nonexistent. They were also dissatisfied with the system of payment for overtime and with the basis on which pay increases were granted. Negative attitudes were also expressed about the number of workers skilled enough to do a good job, the general quality of new union employees, and the morale of employees compared with what it was five years before.

Comments from the supervisors indicated that they did not feel free to express their opinions about issues related to their jobs. These items included decisions on hiring, transfers and promotions of subordinates, and matters related to their own personal growth and advancement.

The group of middle managers surveyed included the titles of director, manager, and superintendent. There were a total of 664 middle-management employees completing the survey.

*Middle managers* expressed highly favorable attitudes about their understanding of company benefits, about the friendly and cooperative people they worked with, and about their belief that concern for air pollution and preservation of the environment was an integral part of their jobs. They wanted to have their performance reviewed annually in a personal interview, and they felt strongly that promotions should be made primarily on merit.

Moderately favorable attitudes were expressed by middle managers toward most aspects of their immediate supervision, most of the benefits provided by the company, job safety, most working conditions, and their freedom to express themselves concerning hiring, dismissals, and new policies. They agreed that top management was concerned with the preservation of the environment and problems of pollution and responsive to the social and economic needs of the community. They felt that most of the people they worked with were sincerely interested in their jobs and worked hard. Most were proud of their association with the company.

Serious dissatisfaction was registered concerning the quality of union workers and top management's handling of union problems. Middle managers felt strongly that promotions should not be made on the basis of seniority.

Dissatisfaction was also expressed over too much overtime and with the system for paying overtime. There was also dissatisfaction strongly indicated about the lack of responsibility delegated to them and the limited authority given them to do their jobs. They also felt that there was too little backup from management on decisions that they made. Dissatisfaction was expressed that there was too much paperwork and report writing required, with too little time for planning. They felt that they should be consulted more about their subordinates in terms of hiring, transfers, and dismissals.

They were also dissatisfied about the amount of clerical and technical help available and the ability of top management to understand the problems of field employees. Another area where they voiced dissatisfaction was with opportunities for promotions. They felt there were not enough promotions from within. They also felt that most managers would not assume more responsibility if it were offered to them.

Presumably, OAS representatives met with the company's top management prior to issuing their final report. This allowed

the company the opportunity to modify or at least soften any results found unfavorable—at a minimum to influence the way in
which the findings were presented.

In reporting the results of the surveys, OAS simply gave tables with the weighted averages of responses to their questions,
the frequency of comments, and an overall summary for each
level of management. They made no attempt to interpret or com-
ment on the data. Presumably their assignment did not include
making recommendations about their findings since there were
none indicated in their reports.

The OAS report was filed away; and it was not circulated
within the company. Why the report was uncirculated is un-
clear: it may have been because top management was not really
interested in what the managers thought, or it may have been
because they knew the report did not represent the true opinions of supervisors. (Supervisors were often afraid to express
themselves for fear of being disciplined or penalized.)

Two years after the company testified at the EEO hearings, it
hired its first visible minority member for a middle-management
staff position. I was hired as an internal consultant and management trainer to implement the company's training programs,
which were just being initiated by a director and a manager in
the department of training and development. These in-house
programs were designed and conducted by the company's staff
of management trainers.

During the *management skills workshops* there was ample opportunity for the supervisors to express their feelings and
attitudes about the company and their jobs. It was through these
workshops that some complaints of company management personnel came to the attention of upper management. The trainers
reported that the supervisors were dissatisfied with some aspects
of their jobs. This was evidenced by many supervisors saying
that they wished they could go back to the union or form their
own supervisory union (supervisory unions were illegal in the
utility). They said that some union employees turned down promotions because they did not want to be in management. They
complained that their bosses undermined their authority by fail-
ing to keep them informed, by going directly to their subordinates to give assignments without their knowledge, and by
overturning decisions they made. They complained that their
bosses failed to delegate authority but blamed them when something went wrong. Related to this were similar complaints about

the strict, autocratic style that their bosses used. The supervisors were not allowed to participate in decision making and were told to "do it or else." (This undoubtedly was exacerbated by the military background of those in top management.) They were especially angry that they "didn't get any backup" on discipline that they meted out to subordinates. Often subordinates who had been laid off without pay were reinstated with pay by the manager or director, much to the supervisor's embarrassment.

Another complaint often heard was that the new union employees were no longer any good. This complaint was frequently made about the JOBS '70s employees. Supervisors told stories about JOBS employees who had tried to hit a supervisor with an axe, who were drug addicts, who did not follow company rules, and so on. They complained that minorities and women received special treatment, which was unfair to regular employees; for example, JOBS employees could not be fired—no matter what they did—and they could not do the jobs for which they were hired. These complaints did not reflect the reality of the situation; there were no skills required for these jobs and JOBS employees could be fired. The complaints reflected the supervisors' feelings and prejudiced attitudes toward the minorities (and JOBS).

Some of the JOBS '70s employees were high school graduates, and some had a year or two of college. It was not true that these employees could not be fired or disciplined if necessary. There were a few supervisors who spoke favorably about their experiences with JOBS subordinates—in contradiction to the other supervisors who said they were all bad.

Although the dissatisfactions expressed by supervisors were not apparent in the OAS survey, it is possible that they did not feel free in the survey to express negative opinions because of the implicit sanctions against critical comments, while in the informal atmosphere of the training self-expression was encouraged. The small group exercises often elicited confidential remarks from the participants about their jobs, and trainers often served as counselors for participants with problems.

## CONSULTANT FLO

Consultant **FLO** was hired by the company in 1974 as a response to several problems. One of the problems was the JOBS '70s program, complaints being registered by union and management employees. Complaints had been made that new minority and

women employees hired through this program were not qualified to handle jobs at the entry level. These complaints had surfaced during the in-house supervisory training workshops,
especially among first- and second-level supervisors.

To recapitulate, supervisors complained that the JOBS employees were not performing their jobs, that they were shown
favoritism because they were minorities, and that they "couldn't
be touched" because they were part of this program. They also
complained that these new employees were ex-convicts or drug
addicts and, in general, were not fit to be company employees.
Even though this was not true (some were college students),
some supervisors perceived them that way and felt that the new
employees were causing poor morale among the other union
workers. Employees from all levels of the company felt that the
hiring of minorities and women through these special programs
was undermining the spirit of the company and the integrity of
the system, since it seemed to them that the new employees did
not have the basic qualifications for the job. This was the reaction
consultants reported of the long-term employees even though
entry-level jobs required no skills and even though the minorities were receiving special training *prior* to starting the job. Previously entry-level employees had not had formal training
before the job but had learned by on-the-job training.

A vice-president felt that management had to address this issue among the employees and believed that the best way to do so
would be to bring in an impartial party who was a professional at
developing criteria to validate the company's selection criteria.

Other problems related to hiring minorities and women had
also come up during the EEOC hearings in 1971. At that time the
company had been asked about its hiring practices and, particularly, about tests given to entry-level applicants. The AVP of employee relations had testified that the company had stopped
using all preemployment tests for entry-level positions. He explained that "we recently issued a corporate policy signed by the
president which struck out all tests which were not validated
and required that no test could be administered without the approval of the vice president of employee relations and then only
after we did validate it."[2] Undoubtedly, concern about validating
tests was intensified by the 1971 case of *Griggs v. Duke Power
Company*, which came before the U.S. Supreme Court. In this case
the Court ruled that job requirements—such as general intelli-

gence tests or a high school education—that have a disparate effect on groups protected by **Title VII** of the Civil Rights Act of 1964 are prima facie proof of discrimination. The burden of proof is then on the employer to show that the requirements are job related and justified by business necessity. All tests must comply with the **EEOC Guidelines on Testing and Selecting Employees**.[3]

The discontinuation of preemployment testing, in part, had given rise to complaints about the new employees being unqualified. There were a few tests given after employment as "part of a validation program in which we are attempting to determine whether the tests are valid to the performance requirements of the job."[4]

Thus the *Griggs* case had a great impact on selection and hiring procedures, especially in the utilities industry. The EEOC Guidelines "prohibit any job qualifications or selection standards which disproportionately screen out individuals in groups protected by Title VII unless they 1) can be significantly related to job performance, and 2) no alternate non-discriminatory standards can be developed to meet requirements shown to be justified by 'business necessity.' "[5] Validation of requirements is necessary where existing selection procedures have a statistically adverse effect on protected groups.

> *Validation is a very specific technical and complex process. . . .* The *Guidelines* require, if feasible, *criterion related validation.* This is a technical term to describe a study which proves that those who score high on a particular test or selection standard generally turn out to be successful on the job, while those who score low usually turn out to be unsuccessful. . . . If such a study is not feasible, the *Guidelines* require evidence of *content validity*—that is, that the test is an actual sample of the work to be done, or *construct validity*—that the test or other standard measures some characteristic clearly needed for the particular job.[6]

Although the company had begun an attempt to validate its selection process, as mentioned back in the EEOC hearings in 1971, it was not until 1974 that they contracted with FLO to develop selection criteria for them. It appears that the FLO consulting program (discussed below) was primarily an attempt to comply with the demands of the *Griggs* case and the Affirmative Action and Equal Employment Opportunity acts while still addressing the issues raised by supervisory and middle-management complaints. Top management was in a squeeze. At one level they were subject to federal prosecution for job discrimination, and at another level they were threatened with the withdrawal of frontline supervisory and middle-management support. They attempted to resolve the problem by employing a consultant who could provide credibility to the managers while satisfying the requirements of the law.

Consultant FLO, like most of the consultant firms that worked there, was brought into the company by middle management with the sanction of top management—that is, an employment manager hired FLO with the sanction of a vice-president. FLO was selected because of their knowledge of the specialty field of *selection criteria* and because the president of the consulting firm had a reputation as an expert—he had been an important witness testifying about employment selection criteria for the EEOC in one of its major cases against AT & T. Although there were many witnesses in the lengthy trial, presumably FLO was influential since the EEOC was successful and FLO was one of the few experts in validation of employment criteria.

The problem presented to the consultant was that the company did not have validated selection criteria that would provide them with "qualified new employees capable of satisfactorily performing and advancing the company."[7] The assignment for the consultant was to develop objective, valid selection criteria for hiring employees for entry-level positions. They were also asked to conduct a seminar on interviewing techniques to teach middle management how to interview prospective employees without using "unwitting or subtle discriminatory procedures."[8]

In response to their assignment, FLO prepared an *Administrative Manual* that explained their approach and how they developed the instruments to be used in the fair selection of employees. The manual included an explanation of what a trait is, how to identify unique traits and levels, how to determine trait measures and threshold points, and how to specify whether an applicant possesses the desired traits.

The approach used by FLO is a method of identifying threshold levels and degrees of those traits that are essential to the satisfactory performance of the unique functions of a job.

After some months of development, the FLO program was implemented and continued to be used for several years. The FLO system was successful in satisfying the EEO laws and, thereby, relieving for a while the pressures from the EEOC about discrimination in hiring practices. It was also successful in getting the approval of supervisors for the new employees who were hired using the FLO system. There were no major complaints as a result of the program being used.

## CONSULTANT BCF

After the oil crisis of 1973 caused rates to increase rapidly, adverse newspaper publicity about management inefficiencies, mounting customer complaints about charges and service, and the suspension of the company's dividends in 1974, it appeared that something was needed to restore public and private confidence in the utility. Therefore, in 1975 the PSC directed that a study be made of the company's management and operations by a firm of independent management consultants. The PSC itself selected the firm to be hired. It chose one of the world's largest and most eminent consulting firms, **BCF**, to conduct the study. BCF, a northeastern company, was known and respected as one of the best consultant groups not only by the business community but also by the consultant community. They employed about 600 professionals within the firm, two thirds of them with doctorates in their field.

BCF's assignment, as determined by the PSC, was to conduct a study of the company's management and operations in two phases: a *diagnostic phase* and a *follow-up phase*. In the diagnostic phase they were to assess the company's problems and report their findings and recommendations. The demand for the consultant was thus not generated internally: it was required by outside regulators. Management could only comply with the demands. Since the company wanted the PSC to look favorably on their requests for rate increases, which came up several times a year, it was in their interest to cooperate fully (at least to appear to do so) with the consultant. This meant, however, that it was the PSC who selected the consultant and who gave the consultant their assignment. Any attempt on the part of the company to negotiate their mission might be viewed as an attempt to restrict their independence. For similar reasons, BCF was told to submit their findings directly to the PSC, with a copy to the company's top management.

Since the company operated in a hierarchical framework, it was inevitable that the employment of a consultant for such an all-inclusive study get sanctioned from the top. Top management, therefore, was the direct contact for the initial entry of the consultant. Although they entered the company through top management, BCF worked with all levels of management in conducting their study and interviews.

The problem presented to the consultant by the PSC was to conduct a study or *management audit* of the company's overall management and operations. Their assignment was to identify potential areas of opportunity for improvement. BCF was to conduct a diagnostic phase of the study and then return for follow-up as the PSC saw fit. Since BCF was conducting a management audit, they did not need to have the company present them with the problems; they went in to explore for themselves and make their own diagnosis.

BCF used a combined *people and task approach* with, however, an *emphasis on people*, as **S. R. Ganesh** described the approach.[9] This meant that their style had an emphasis on individuals and groups and a concern for employees' feelings and the relationships that they had with the consultant. They believed that people's perceptions were important to getting the job done. There also was an emphasis on cooperation and open communication generated by trust relationships rather than by authority.

BCF interviewed individual managers throughout the organization. To get broad-based data, interviews were done in a *vertical slice*. This meant taking a representative sample of each level of management from first-line supervisor to vice-president and of each major department and division in the company; in some cases, the president and chairman were interviewed, too.

BCF adopted the role of the professional consultants in their interaction with employees. They came in with the reputation of being experts in management and did not try to curry favor or endorsement from the groups with whom they worked. Yet they were concerned about gaining information and gathering the opinions of others in the company. They were cooperative while maintaining a distance. Ganesh's description, using the imagery of a catalyst, fits BCF quite well:

> Their involvement is often used to send a piece of information through the system where the system cannot send the piece of information by itself. . . . I don't have any particular sense of membership in that company or any close attachment, but I know and they know that I'm always available for whatever kind of activity they want, and that I know them well enough that if there is anything important then it might be well for them to call me on it. . . . So I'm an available resource.[10]

As a result of their study, BCF issued a report to the PSC with a copy to the chairman (CEO) of the company. In the report they gave their findings concerning management and operations of the company.

A long-term effort at improvement, BCF felt, was beyond the direct control of company management and was "dependent on the cooperation of state and city governments and influential citizen groups."[11] BCF recognized that progress in company performance was related to

> fundamental new problems confronting all public utility managements, particularly those . . . whose revenues arise primarily from supplying electric service. . . . [The company] is faced not only by the industry-wide challenges but also has to cope with a set of special problems stemming from its own particular location, service area, existing physical facilities and prior management history.[12]

BCF reported, "In the face of these circumstances the company's management has proven itself adept at dealing with the company's operating problems, particularly those amenable to technological/engineering solutions."[13]

Some of the areas mentioned in the report that required improvements were the company's management style, training and development of managers, and cost reduction.

One item that BCF saw as an opportunity for improvement within the company's control was in the area of efficiency and cost reduction. Specifically, BCF stated that considerable savings could be made by a reduction in the supervisory and management staff.[14] By examining company records, BCF determined that the company was top-heavy in management—that is, there were too many managers for the number of workers supervised. Overall, the company's management-to-worker ratio was one manager for every four workers—unusually high for most industries.

Technically, BCF found the utility to be doing as well as could be expected with the limited capital and high costs built into their system (for example, aging physical plants). BCF recommended that a basic change in management style be made to improve the performance of the company. This required setting overall corporate goals and the regular development of short- and long-term plans. It also required "more focused and clear-cut objectives throughout the company and then measuring performance against the agreed-upon objectives." This, it was expected, would lead to "far-reaching improvements in management effectiveness" and, ultimately, "to improved financial and operating performance of the company."[15]

An issue about management style was that the company had a number of top executives who came from military backgrounds. BCF found that the company was indeed drawing too much from a military source for its recruitment of managers. This also intensified the problem of developing managers with broad-based management experience, since most of management's present experience was of a military nature. BCF specifically noted:

> It is worth acknowledging here the frequent comments (and implied criticism) that have been made regarding the number of former military men brought in. The number is obviously, in relative terms, high. Given the need for immediate action, it is understandable that the Chairman would look for management resources among those groups with which he had prior contacts and experience, e.g., the government and the military establishment.[16]

Although BCF did not state that this was detrimental per se, they did "question the desirability of too much concentration of any one type of background, training and experience, especially if it compounds an already existing imbalance."[17]

Some management consultants, BCF among them, have adopted the theory that a healthy organization has many management styles working as complements in the company. This is in keeping with leadership research that shows that no one style is suitable for all situations. A variety of styles also helps avoid "groupthink," which may lead to poor decision making because of the loss of critical thinking. **Irving Janis** describes the symptoms of groupthink exhibited as shared stereotypes, rationalizations, the illusion of invulnerability, unanimity, and direct pressure applied to anyone who speaks out with doubts.[18] In their specific recommendations, BCF recommended that "top management . . . initiate a modification in its management style."[19]

This recommendation was based on the disadvantages of the autocratic style, which is epitomized in the military. With this style the superior tells the subordinate what to do, and the subordinate must comply without questioning. The subordinate does not participate in the decision-making process and must adhere strictly, without deviation from standard policies. Disobedience or deviation from instructions can, and usually does, produce severe reaction from the superiors in the form of punishment, often without regard to the seriousness of the infraction. **Robert Jackall** refers to the effects that an organizational restructuring can have when a new person is named CEO—as was the case when the new chairman began in this company. He states that the crucial feature is that the "shakeup rearranges the fealty structure . . . placing those in power who mesh with the CEO in style and public image."[20] Thus the managers' desire to get promoted causes them to accommodate to whatever is officially sanctioned. This tends, in the autocratic style, to stifle innovation and initiative, which are vital to the company in coping with changes and external pressures.

Another area where the company was found lacking was in the development of its management staff. Company managers were found to be technically strong but weak in their overall management ability. This was because most managers in the company had come up through the ranks, sometimes within one department. This, naturally, had limited their exposure and experience as managers. It was not unusual for someone to be promoted from union to management with no management training at all. In addition, BCF found that lower-level managers were not being given the chance to grow and develop because their supervisors were not delegating authority or allowing participation in decision making (these are other aspects of the autocratic management style). BCF recommended "initiation of a personnel development program aimed at improving the managerial skills of . . . staff at both the executive and supervisory levels. At the same time, attention should be given to the re-evaluation and clarification of the roles of managerial position, including the associated level of decision-making authority."[21]

Another reason why development of internal management talent was critical was that the company lacked "broadly-based general management talent."[22] This came about because officers who had been in the company in 1967—at the time the current chairman took office—retired by 1973. Other experienced personnel also retired during that period. This unusual depletion of top management stemmed from the mergers without layoffs, which were occurring during the company's expansionist period. This created a "hump" in the normal age distribution curve. For a number of years, therefore, people were not promoted to high-level management positions until they reached an advanced age. Furthermore, the reduction of the mandatory retirement age from 68 to 65 in 1967 accelerated the loss. Attempts to hire outside managers with broad utility experience were only partly successful because many were not willing to move to the city or to undertake the task of working with the well-known problems of the company.[23] As an additional aid in the development of management, BCF recommended the establishment of an *internal consulting capability.*

*Management development programs* were also necessary because many company managers had a great deal of technical knowledge but little experience in general management. Management training in the company had only recently been initiated. Such development was also needed in response to complaints from lower-level managers that they were not being consulted about decisions that affected them or allowed to participate in the decision-making process.

These findings substantiated the criticisms of leadership style and management that had been made by both internal (lower management) and external (customers, government agencies, and the PSC) forces—and on which the news media had focused sharply.

The implications of the BCF report were felt in several areas. Initially, the report prompted the company to issue its own report commenting on the BCF findings and recommendations. They said that they did not understand some of the "broad general recommendations" and conclusions—for example, the one on management style. Accordingly, they held a meeting with BCF representatives, with members of the PSC sitting in as observers, to "seek enlightenment" from BCF. The company was not satisfied, however, with the responses to their questions. They asked for information to support the observations, recommendations, and comments in the BCF report. They claimed that the BCF representatives were unable to supply them with the necessary information; BCF had agreed to get it for them as soon as they could. According to an executive, BCF reneged on this promise by telling them that "it would be undesirable for them to supply us information in support of their conclusions,"[24] even though the company claimed to be seeking only information that would permit them to understand, evaluate, and respond to the report.

The company complained that because their relationship with BCF was not the "typical process of management consulting," in that the BCF findings were not reviewed by the company while still in draft form, "as would normally be the case," this placed a great limitation on the process. This arrangement was established by the PSC and accepted by the company and the consultant to establish the independence and impartiality of the report.[25] The company believed, however, that this limitation placed a "special duty on the consultants to verify their findings and support their recommendations by full investigation at all appropriate levels of management and to refrain from indulging in conjectural assumptions and unsupported conclusions."[26] They felt that BCF failed to do this. The company appeared to be dissatisfied with BCF's work and resistant to some of its findings; yet the influence that the report would have with the PSC required at least some acquiescence.

Two years later, the BCF report was still having an indirect impact, as it contributed to the firing of 211 managers in March of

1977. Many people in the company felt that an AVP, in response to the complaints of inefficiency and to external pressures to take action, and feeling justified by the BCF report that had indicated that the company was top-heavy in management, decided to fire 211 managers. This was historic because the company had always been a secure place to work, similar to the civil service in that once a person worked there for a while he could not get fired except under extreme circumstances. Employees usually came to the company directly out of school and worked their way up the corporate ladder until retirement. Even during times when cutbacks in personnel had been necessary, traditionally they were accomplished by attrition rather than by layoffs. Sometimes this resulted in employees who were not performing well being retained on the job, aggravating the "deadwood" problem and the high-slack organization of the company.

Some employees felt that this drastic action was taken by the AVP to demonstrate to the public and to the PSC that the company was taking action to solve their management problems (in this case, excessive management personnel). It was also felt that the decision to fire the 211 was influenced by the company's desire to try to quell the outraged voices that generally arise when a request for a rate increase is impending before the PSC, as it was in 1976. The company, it was alleged, thought that it would make their case look better if they could show that they "trimmed" their management staff.

The immediate impact of the firing, however, was disastrous. The morale in the company was severely damaged because those managers who remained on the job felt their security threatened. Rumors were rampant. Some departments were left without an administrator to coordinate and give them direction. In addition, an EEO class action suit was filed by some of those fired, charging the company with age discrimination under the *Age Discrimination in Employment Act of 1967*. This act specifies that it is unlawful for an employer to "fail or refuse to hire or to discharge any individual or otherwise discriminate against any individual with respect to his compensation, terms, conditions or privileges of employment because of such individual's age."[27]

The age discrimination charges, which have still not been adjudicated, came about because of the way in which the managers to be fired were selected. Two months prior to the firings, every

department had been told to identify through performance rat-
ings the best managers in their area.  The rationale given at the
time for doing this was that it was an effort to reward the top 5
percent in performance and potential by giving them special
training opportunities. Later, when department heads were told
to identify their bottom 5 percent, no directive was given on
how to select them. Thus objective criteria  based on performance were not used in identifying poor managers, and the criteria that were used were not consistent across departments. Some
departments used seniority, some used performance, and some
made their decisions on the basis of expedience or individual
preferences. The only consistent characteristic of those selected
as "bottoms" was overwhelmingly: age. Preferences served to
overrepresent older managers on the bottoms list. Yet more than
75 percent of this group had received the top performance rating
on their annual review. The older managers therefore filed an age
discrimination suit claiming they were illegally terminated on
the basis of age.

Lastly, another consequence of the BCF findings was that the
company felt a need to bring in additional consultants to help
provide management development programs and to improve its
management. As a result, several consultants—such as consultants ABC, CRY, and BPA—were brought into the organization in
the mid-1970s.

## CONSULTANT ABC

The complaints about the company's excessively autocratic **leadership style** had come to the attention of management from several sources. The first attitude survey conducted by OAS in 1971
reported that some managers felt that they were not consulted
about decisions that affected them and their subordinates. During the company's management training workshops, complaints
had also surfaced in which lower-level managers said that their
bosses did not ask for their input on decisions, did not allow
them to make their own decisions, and were punitive when they
made mistakes. In addition, they felt that the opportunities for
growth and promotion were limited. These problems of managerial style were somewhat confirmed by the BCF report, which,

however, did not document the complaint in detail. BCF recommended that the company "initiate a modification in its management style,"[28] which tended to be predominantly military.

One of the alleged consequences of the autocratic style is the lack of opportunities for the continuous development of managers because lower-level managers are not allowed to participate in decision making and must go up the chain of command for decisions. This can be a problem in an emergency when an immediate decision must be made; yet even here the manager is likely to wait for his superior to tell him what to do. Situations like this had occurred too often in the company. For example, during the 1965 blackout delayed action on the part of those in the control room caused the blackout to spread throughout the city.

The lack of sufficient management development was also cited by BCF as a problem. Managers often lacked the experience for promotions because they were barely permitted to do their own jobs, let alone learn others. Superiors did not usually trust subordinates to make important decisions. In addition, the autocratic style can restrict decision making and inhibit creativity. With changes occurring rapidly, the company now felt it needed another style of leadership that would be more suitable to the accommodation of change.

Thus when consultant **ABC** presented their program, the company embraced it as an opportunity to address both the recommendations for more *management training* and the problem of *leadership styles* at the same time, as ABC had a workshop on leadership styles for managers.

Consultant ABC's initial contact with the company was made at a national training meeting where the president of ABC was conducting a workshop. The workshop was about leadership styles—identifying nonproductive behavior and behavior that is appropriate in a variety of situations. A company trainer attended the workshop, was impressed with what he saw, and thereafter sought out the consultant. At first the company trainer confided in the consultant about some problems that he thought were occurring in the company: lack of direction in the company, in-house fighting among several groups in the department, and the problems that were caused by the AVP's style. ABC's president gave the trainer some strategies to try and said that he thought the company would benefit from the type of management workshop his consultant firm could provide. The consultant was also able to help the trainer with a personal problem. This served to establish a personal relationship between the two. Shortly thereafter, the consultant was invited to meet the director and the AVP. The presentation he made about his program on leadership styles was warmly received, and soon after the consultant was hired.

Top management felt that its leadership-style problem would only be exacerbated by the influx of minorities and women because the minorities would be antagonistic to the **underutilizations** and **concentrations**[29] that the company had been enforcing. Concentrations in some jobs and departments reflected stereotypes of these ethnic groups in the society at large. For example, at that time the motor pool in the company was entirely male and almost entirely black, while the construction department was the province of Italian Americans. The Irish Americans comprised the various electrical units in the company.

These ethnic monopolies in various areas of the company had not been initially formed on the basis of usurpation; it was both a natural progression due to the fact that certain ethnic immigrants were available historically for such work and a result of their prior training and experience in their homelands as well as elsewhere in the city. The Irish were available for leadership positions in the company because they came from an English-speaking country; therefore, their transition was not as difficult as transition would be for non-English-speaking groups. The Irish also preceded the other ethnic groups in the company. This and other advantages enabled them to move into operations positions that required reading of gauges and recording of numbers.

Consequently, ABC was brought into the company to help reduce both the existing friction and that which was anticipated when blacks and other minorities were to be upgraded under affirmative action requirements. The AVP decided that the consultant could help the company moderate its leadership style by showing managers the rewards of other leadership styles in specific situations.

ABC's assignment was to train and certify the company's internal trainers to teach a standardized, leadership-style workshop, which ABC had designed. Certification meant that ABC would teach the company's trainers how to conduct their workshop, then license them as official ABC instructors empowered to teach the ABC training program in any company. ABC would conduct the first workshops with company trainers as observers and then coach the company trainers when they did the program the first time themselves. At first there was some resistance on the part of the company trainers to the consultant because the trainers had serious reservations about the ethics of ABC's program. They felt that the program psychologically manipulated managers. ABC was able to overcome the initial resistance through the licensing procedure, which would enhance the trainers' professionalism. ABC also related to the trainers as colleagues—fellow "cosmopolitans" who had mutual professional goals, which further enhanced their acceptance by the staff.

ABC's services centered around a few workshops that were all based on the same model. Built on Maslow's need hierarchy, the workshops emphasized the impact of secondary needs (esteem, belongingness, independence, and so on) on behavior. When these secondary needs became operational, after primary needs for pay and fringe benefits had been essentially met, they gave rise to specific motives; that is, drives to satisfy needs. Behavior is the manifestation of these motives.

The consultant's adaptation of Maslow's need hierarchy schema was used to evaluate and systematically chart situational behavior by examining four factors in managerial interactions between manager and peer, manager and subordinate, and manager and superior.

ABC's style was people oriented, as described by Ganesh. The style involved an emphasis on individuals and groups and not on structure. It stressed concern for others' feelings and the relationships that individuals have with each other and the consultant. The people-oriented approach focuses on personal relationships as the most important aspect of a well-functioning organization. The emphasis is on getting along with others, on trust, and on open communication.

ABC demonstrated their people approach by the way the firm's president entered the company. The president of ABC was able to come into the company by establishing a personal relationship with one of the company's management trainers. As described previously, the relationship began at the training conference where the two met and was continued by telephone. The trainer confided personal problems to the consultant and their relationship continued along personal lines. Even after ABC entered the company, the president continued to establish personal relationships with company members who confided information on problems that they felt were detrimental to the organization.

For example, ABC's president was informed about the situation with the new AVP who had caused difficulty for the company by some ill-chosen words to minority vendors. This outburst became a source of embarrassment to his immediate superior, the vice-president, as well as to the chairman of the board. The vice-president wished to retaliate for the pressure he was getting from groups within the company and from outraged minority groups outside the company. Knowing that the AVP was the sort of individual who would behave in a hasty fashion and "let the chips fall where they may"—and in accordance with his pattern on the behavioral grid as suggested by ABC's module— the AVP was given the responsibility for firing the excessive personnel. After the firing of the 211 (as described earlier) created a furor in the company, the AVP was asked to resign. In this way top management in the company was able to use the knowledge learned from the consultant for its own internal political aims. Such information is usually not presented to an outside consultant. It may well be that the president used personal charm, influence, and contacts (including personal advice) to gain official entry into the company. The manager may have responded to the charm and advice to employ him for official activities that were primarily related to his personal characteristics.

ABC also demonstrated their people approach by working with individuals and groups in their training sessions. Throughout their relationships, they stressed the need for being candid and trusting others. This approach reflected the fact that the founder of ABC was a clinical psychologist.

As mentioned earlier, prior to the entry of this consultant, all departments had been asked to identify their top 5 percent of managers (as noted above). The company proposed that ABC's program be given as a special reward for those identified as the most promising managers. When the program was introduced, departments were told that only the "cream of the crop" could attend. In addition, department heads were told that the program was so special that no interruptions during the training sessions would be allowed. This, in principle, would make the top 5 percent into an obvious elite. What in fact occurred, however, was that during an ABC workshop of middle managers a manager was called out of the program by his supervisor and told that he was being demoted—in direct contradiction to the policy of sending the top 5 percent to the session and of not interrupting the program while it was in progress.

Another outcome, totally unintended, was that the implementation of the instructor training for the workshops was a precipitating factor leading to an EEO suit being filed.

The ABC program was supposed to be stimulating managers to use other styles of management rather than relying on the autocratic and hierarchical style as had been traditionally done. Instead, the very fact of making it into an elite program tended to confirm the hierarchical tendencies in the organization. In that way it adopted a democratic model of managerial training, which the company negated. Once having done so, they violated their own policy by eliminating senior managers. The policy of choosing only the elite for training apparently came into conflict with the policy of training for democratic management. The head of the management training section had told the training staff that they must participate in the ABC instructor training. When one of the trainers was unable to attend the first session, the individual was threatened with the loss of his job. The democratic ideology was again being implemented in an arbitrary manner. When this autocratic style was brought to the attention of management as being contrary to the ABC teachings, the section head responded, "The ABC theory is fine, but you know how it is out there in the real world." Higher management sustained the training head. As a result the trainer who did not participate was penalized by having a promotion withheld that had already been promised in writing. Shortly thereafter, he filed an EEO suit, charging the company with discrimination for denying him the promotion.

The firing of the 211 managers occurred about seven months later, and the head of one of the training sections was one of those fired. In spite of the fact that he had the top rating on his performance review, he was told that his "management style was not suitable" for the company. As described earlier, his firing led to the filing of a class action EEO suit that charged the company with age discrimination. In addition, since the position of section head was not filled, there was no one to give direction, make decisions, or provide stimulation for the section. Within the year all but one member of the section had resigned. The ABC program continued for another few months and then was discontinued. There were no apparent changes in the leadership or management style in the company.

## CONSULTANT CRY

Another area where consultants were used was in the Construction and Maintenance Department in one of the company divisions. The use of the consultant began with the need to have a hard, objective financial policy. In 1974 the company began to experience a serious shortage of capital and no growth in sales. By 1976 the decision was made to spend no money on construction or repairs except those needed to maintain service—that is, if something broke, it would be repaired. This measure resulted in less work for the construction department. Some of its personnel were transferred to other departments or placed on other assignments. In this climate consultant **CRY** was introduced in 1976. Another reason for bringing CRY into the company was to try to satisfy a recommendation of the BCF report that mentioned the need to develop a system to record and report working time.

CRY entered the organization through a contact on the middle-management level, a division director. CRY employed the son of another director as one of its staff consultants. It was through this personal contact that the relationship with the company was established. The head of CRY was a well-known political figure, having been a gubernatorial candidate. Thus CRY was selected not because of experience or expertise, but because of a personal relationship and the political contacts it offered. CRY also had visibility and prestige owing to its reputation for successful work in one large corporation.

The problem directed to the consultant was defined and evaluated by middle management, first by the division director and later by the training manager. The managers who hired CRY were the same ones who presented the problem to them. The problem, as mentioned in the BCF report, was that there was no formal, recorded system for reporting work and time to upper management so that they could be informed about work progress. At the end of each day, field-workers would tell their supervisor what was done or what problems they had encountered. Beyond the informal, verbal report, upper management had no way of telling how long a job should take or how much time (or money) was being spent on a job. This information was needed so that better planning could be undertaken for the long range. In addition, there were no controls nor a master plan against which work could be checked and monitored. The consultant's assignment was to develop a *planning* and *scheduling system* for this department.

Although CRY entered the organization with a personal contact, their approach and style in working in the department was very much that of task orientation. This meant that they were not concerned about their relationships with employees but with the task itself and the organization of work. They emphasized getting the job done and looked at the reporting system as the key to maintaining efficiency. They approached the problem as a deficiency in the overall system in which information and controls were needed to ensure responsibility. They did not consider the effect that the system would have on the people working there.

They saw themselves as experts who were hired because of their knowledge in developing reporting and control systems. When they came into the department, they felt no need to establish personal relationships with department members. Since they had the sanction of upper management, they had the leverage to get the information they needed for their assignment without developing any rapport with the employees. In the time they spent in the company, little of it was spent eliciting opinions and input from any of the people affected by their system.

The manifest outcome was the development of a Planning and Scheduling System that allowed for the reporting of work and short-term scheduling. The system reported the amount of work done and the time spent on each project and by each employee and provided periodic printouts of what had been accomplished weekly compared with overall monthly and six-month plans.

Another result of CRY's system was that a committee was formed made up of members of various departments who would be involved with implementing the system. In spite of the committee, CRY left the department with many problems in the implementation of the system. CRY had done no implementation or training for using its system. No one in the division knew how to use the forms or understood what the numbers meant. Resentment was rampant because of the increase in paperwork that the system entailed, especially among the field-workers. The mechanics of the forms themselves were beyond the level of many of the employees. Many did not have the mathematical skills to compute the averages in decimals, as was required. In addition, the system was seen as threatening because in the situation where their jobs were not secure owing to the shortage of work, they were now required to report in their time on paper and to account for every hour of their workday.

Comparisons were also to be made among employees as to the amount of work they were accomplishing. Standards had been established for the amount of time a job should take. Each area also had an average that represented the "normal" amount of work that was expected to be produced. If an employee's average was too low, the supervisor was expected to do something to improve the worker's output. The workers feared that their jobs might be in jeopardy; if their statistics did not look good, they might get fired. The system itself exacerbated the already low morale in the department.

As far as productivity, although the author was not present when the system was in operation, results from other companies who used the CRY system have been published. **Business Week** reports that although the system results in an immediate productivity increase after installing the system, later on productivity plummets "as workers rebel against what they believe is a tyrannical approach to production quotas." Although CRY insists that the system is an effective tool, "other consultants complain that some of [CRY's] former clients have been so turned off by the experience with the technique that they have now closed their doors to virtually all consultants."[30]

The company, meanwhile, continued to use outside consultants to implement the CRY system and to address the morale and climate problems created by CRY. Consultant BPA, a completely people-oriented organization development group, was hired to improve morale and to help the internal staff implement the system of planning and scheduling in a more democratic way.

## NOTES

1. OAS Report 1971, p. 1.

2. U.S., Equal Employment Opportunity Commission (EEOC), *Hearings before the United States Equal Employment Opportunity Commission on Utilization of Minority and Women Workers in the Public Utilities Industry* (Washington, D.C.: Government Printing Office, November 15, 1971), p. 21.

3. Richard Peres, *Dealing with Employment Discrimination* (New York: McGraw-Hill, 1974), p. 54.

4. U.S., EEOC, *Hearings*, p. 20.

5. U.S., EEOC, *Affirmative Action and Equal Employment: A Guidebook for Employers*, vol. 1 (Washington, D.C.: Government Printing Office, 1974), p. 35.

6. Ibid., p. 36.

7. The Company Affirmative Action Report, 1973.

8. Ibid.

9. S. R. Ganesh, "Organizational Consultants: A Comparison of Styles," *Human Relations* 31 (1978): 7.

10. Ibid., p. 16.

11. BCF Report, 1975, p. 4.

12. Ibid.

13. Ibid.

14. Ibid., p. 39.

15. Ibid., p. 5.

16. Ibid., p. 43.

17. Ibid.

18. Irving Janis, *Victims of Groupthink* (Boston: Houghton Mifflin, 1972).

19. BCF Report, "Recommendations," p. 9.

20. Robert Jackall, "Moral Mazes: Bureaucracy and Managerial Work," *Harvard Business Review*, in press.

21. BCF Report, "Recommendations," p. 11.

22. BCF Report, p. 6.

23. Comments by the Company on the BCF Report, 1975, p. 23.

24. Ibid., pp. 12–13.

25. BCF Report, p. 2.

26. Comments by the Company, p. 14.

27. Peres, *Dealing with Employment Discrimination*, p. 285.

28. BCF Report, "Recommendations," p. 9.

29. *Underutilization* is defined as "having fewer minorities or women in a particular job category than would reasonably be expected by their presence in the relevant labor market. It also means employing persons in jobs that do not make adequate use of their skills and training. 'Concentration' means more of a particular group in a job category or department than would reasonably be expected by their presence in the workforce." EEOC, *Affirmative Action and Equal Employment*, pp. 23–24.

30. "The New Shape of Management Consulting," *Business Week*, May 21, 1979, p. 104.

# PART III
# Conclusion

# F I V E

# Summary and Discussion

## SUMMARY

A basic theory underlying modern organizations is that to succeed they must act in rational and effective ways. This analysis of the various management consultants hired to aid the organization in realizing its goals suggests that many actions related to the consultancy do not contribute to the solution of the overall problems of the organization. Further, many of the results of the consultancy created side effects, or latent effects, that differ in consequence from the original statements of the manifest goals.

There is also the issue of the consultant's role with respect to the client organization. Although the management consultant is employed to provide an objective viewpoint of the client's problem, the consultant must also be loyal to his own employer, the consulting firm, in which he is encouraged to continually generate new business. Without necessarily being dishonest, management consultants may act in such a way that, inadvertently, problems are not resolved. The consultant may not be aware of the entire situation within the organization or the internal politics that will affect the solution that is implemented. It is also possible that because of the social science problems in which the management consultant specializes, which are by nature complex, there are no simple, clear-cut solutions. It is easier to obtain closure on problems brought to consultants dealing with time and motion studies, production engineering, and quality control because of the quantifiable nature of the solutions or the existence of other clear-cut criteria of success or failure. For the social scientist entering industry, strategies and training approaches can legitimately lead to new complications and justify extended consultant involvement. The consultant can only attempt to apply social science theories that have been generated by previous laboratory research to real situations on the assumption that their application will create the same effects produced in the laboratory.

As can be seen from the analysis of the management consultants in this case study, the management consultants in the client utility either had no impact or produced unintended consequences, usually of a negative type. In some instances tools or techniques based on social science theory have been taken by the client company and used for its own political purposes. Rather than being used to implement genuine changes, consultants have helped to enhance the company image, to pacify dissenters within the company, and to satisfy or put off external agencies who were exerting pressures on the company. This study has examined these realities underlying management consulting and their political manifestations.

As a conclusion this chapter will provide a brief recapitulation of the findings of the five management consultants presented in the case study as well as a discussion of the implications of the theories of Merton, Schein, Argyris, Baritz, and Ganesh on the effectiveness of the consultants.

As organizations have grown and changed within their complex environments, they have increasingly turned to industrial experts to broaden their competence and expertise. Yet the external consultants sometimes create more problems than they solve in the organizations that engage them. An in-depth study of the five consultants within one company was undertaken (1) to determine whether or not and how or how not they benefited or injured the client organization and (2) to examine the unintended consequences of their interventions.

Although management consulting began in relatively narrow and specific areas within a small number of industries, it has broadened and become widespread. Management consulting originated in industry as an application and outgrowth of engineering and technical knowledge. **Frederick Taylor**—one of the first management consultants—began with the intention of increasing productivity in the steel industry, and **Lillian Gilbreth** combined the interest in efficiency with the human aspects of workers. Time and motion studies were done with little attention to any other worker needs. **Hugo Munsterberg** provided organizational assistance by testing for worker selection to ensure that the worker would be able to perform the desired task.

**Elton Mayo** again considered issues of worker productivity in conducting the *Hawthorne experiments*. For him the solution lay in paying greater attention to the workers' social needs.

**Chester Barnard** referred to the necessity of communicating with and getting the cooperation of the employees, as the employees' needs came to be recognized more and more as contributing to productivity. The emphasis changed, therefore, from the *scientific management approach* of authoritarian or hierarchical management, with tangible incentives as the way to achieve organization goals, to the more indirect *participative management approaches*, which emphasized the socio-psychological needs of employees to achieve organization goals.

The emphasis on worker needs culminated with the *human relations approach*, which stressed motivation, leadership, and worker participation as means to achieve good morale and thereby increase productivity. Although the idea that a happy worker is a more productive worker was eventually discredited, the influence of the human relations school remained.

The concern with motivation expanded into many theories, some emphasizing job satisfaction. **Herzberg's** and **Maslow's** theories were used to examine workers' secondary needs as a means to improve productivity. In attempts to increase output, many companies employed Herzberg's techniques to give workers more responsibility.

Along with the emphasis on motivation came the realization among management consultants that a different type of leadership style was required to elicit the most from workers in a participative management style. The authoritarian or hierarchical style did not allow workers to participate, so that *democratic* or *shared authority* came into favor. Because research has shown that no one style is effective in all situations, the democratic style is no longer exclusively considered to be the best. It is interesting to note, however, that most companies have not made this transition to style flexibility and are still using one style consistently. Such was the case in the client organization cited in the case study. In that company the predominant leadership style was autocratic or hierarchical, stemming in part from the military background of many of the company's top executives.

In this case the use of consultants to change management's style of leadership was not successful in making an impact on the company's functioning. The major technique used by consultants in trying to change leadership style is the **management training workshop**. Although research on the effectiveness of leadership training has shown it to be of questionable value (that is, no definitive effects have been demonstrated), management consultants, and companies with their own trainers, still employ this technique at great expense. In the case study, while consultants were hired to bring new management techniques to the company, the organization, in effect, was not willing to permit changes in the company functioning.

In the relatively small amount of literature written about management consultants, the consensus is that management consultants are used in industry as change agents, diagnosticians, or problem solvers. The main attraction of the consultant is that he offers objectivity—by virtue of being an outsider—or expertise that the organization does not itself have. The consultant can also provide a third-party view or mediate a political situation within the company.

Criticism of consultants usually centers around complaints that they overcharge clients, that they lose their objectivity by becoming involved in the company, and that the consultant firm serves its own interests foremost, rather than the client's.

Suggestions to help reduce the likelihood of developing problems with consultants emphasize the need to be specific in the statement of written commitment as to what the consultant firm will do and how it will do it. Yet these suggestions deal only with the **manifest problems** in the consultant's relationship with the client. There is little attention paid to the various underlying **latent problems** and the hidden motives that cause clients to hire consultants. As seen in the case study, in most of the relationships with the consultants, the **presenting problem** was merely tangentially related to the reasons the client was using management consultants.

**William Reddin** pointed out some of the common errors that consultants make in their relationships with client companies. In the case study many of the errors listed by Reddin were illustrated. These include creating change overload, raising expectations, allowing inappropriate attachment, and losing professional detachment. For example, in the case study the OAS survey raised the expectations of lower-level managers that there would be changes; yet top management made none. CRY produced change overload by developing a system that the division was unprepared or unable to implement. ABC made the errors of establishing inappropriate attachment and losing professional detachment by becoming personally involved with a few members of the company.

**Ganesh** emphasized the style of the consultant as a mediator on the effectiveness of his application of social science theory to organizations. He divided styles and approaches into two main categories: people oriented and task oriented. The people orientation has a human relations approach that values personal, interpersonal, and group aspects, while the task orientation has a systematic approach that values issues that affect the whole organization and patterns of work and systems.

**Merton's** concept of *manifest* and *latent function* is particularly relevant to this study. With this concept behaviors that would otherwise have been termed *irrational*—since they do not contribute to overt or manifest goals—become more comprehensible when identified as being latent functions, which are not publicly stated but which lead to unintended though observable consequences. Actual functions within an organization include the manifest as well as the latent functions. The problem here and elsewhere is to pinpoint these latent functions and intentions.

Other types of latent functions include political activities within the organization stemming from personal or work-related motives for power acquisition. The resultant behavior is usually deceptive in that it often cannot be publicly recognized and helps support the illusion that the organization is functioning in another fashion. These may contribute to organizational goals either by being work related or by providing personal satisfaction to employees, which induces them to stay in an otherwise boring environment. The acquisition of personal power as the basis of a latent function can be seen to flourish in the high-slack organization, since there is little competition and plenty of time to spend on personal goals without disrupting the system.

The organization in the case study is a typical high-slack environment. It operated in a fairly stable environment and required routine functions even among management. Personal power acquisition was frequently seen in the company.

Classical theory of management builds on the **bureaucratic model**. This concern with functions and principles has been assailed as being unresponsive to human needs. **Argyris** claims that by concentrating solely on function the organization itself causes subordinate dependence and alienation. An organization that fails to encourage or support individual autonomy and motivation can ultimately expect to be an inflexible or unresponsive organization.

Argyris describes a model of the organization that can serve both individual and organizational goals in terms of the science of values (*axiology*). The axiologically good organization is one in which there is an interrelationship among the parts of the organization, an awareness of a pattern created by the parts, and an influence over internal and external activities. There is effective problem solving and an awareness of past history and future events as well as present concerns in considering the goals and activities of the organization.

The case study presented here is an example of an axiologically not-good organization in that there is little apparent interrelationship among the parts. Even within departments one section had no knowledge of what another section was doing. This was well illustrated by the training and development department where a consultant was called in to work with a division and the other sections knew nothing about it until one of their clients happened to mention it. The head of the department claimed that he maintained this lack of awareness among sections for organizational goals; he claimed it fostered a competitive atmosphere. In many cases divisions within the company acted independently without regard for other divisions or departments. Problem solving was not effective, and there was a tendency to look at problems in the short term rather than considering their long-range effects. The axiologically not-good nature of the organization was also demonstrated by the emphasis on hierarchical control rather than concern for the members who made up the various parts of the organization. There was no opportunity for autonomy or independence if one wanted to remain in favor with management.

**Kast**, while noting the conflict between organizational structure and worker satisfaction of needs, suggests that the organization should not deal with the individual's need for status, growth, and independence to increase job satisfaction, since personal fulfillment comes from many sources in the sociocultural environment, often outside of management's control. **Dubin** echoes a similar view when he observes that work may not be the central life interest of some employees. He feels that management should concentrate on other means of attaining productivity rather than appealing to higher-order needs on the job.

**William Kornhauser** sees a conflict between professional demands and the demands of the organization. Each influences the other; the organization has become more influenced by professional standards of expertise, autonomy, and responsibility; the professional has become more subject to bureaucratic and organizational controls. On the other hand, there are built-in strains when a scientist works for an organization. The social scientist who enters the organization with a background in human relations and motivation theory may find conflict with hierarchical controls.

**Alvin Gouldner**, utilizing Merton's concept of manifest and latent to the roles of the professional, applied Merton's distinction between *cosmopolitans* and *locals* to management. The cosmopolitans maintain professional standards and lean toward outside values. The locals place the values and goals of the organization above those of their profession. In terms of the case study, one might expect that the company—partially because of its inbreeding—might be composed largely of locals, while the consultants would at least begin with a more cosmopolitan view. This outlook served to create bonds between the consultants with a cosmopolitan perspective and those members of the company who also shared the professional view. This relationship of one professional to another, in some instances, helped the consultant to be more readily accepted by the company's staff. For example, ABC was able to overcome resistance from the training staff by appealing to their professional aspirations.

Consultants are hired on the basis of their professional expertise and objectivity. Yet this may become compromised by exposure to the client over a period of time and the professional standards relaxed by the desire to continue providing consultant services.

**Baritz** regards the social scientist as having given up his professionalism by allowing his knowledge of the control of human behavior to be used by management at the expense of workers. He proposes that the social scientist has lost his objectivity and critical analysis by accepting the norms of the dominant elite in industry. **Radom**, however, disputes this and maintains that social scientists have retained their autonomy and professionalism. He believes that their position as social scientists has placed them in a more influential role than the physical scientists in that they are involved in policy making and are thus able to ensure that organizational goals do not conflict with their professional goals. The case study, however, tends to support Baritz's contention that the social scientist's knowledge and techniques have, often unwittingly, been used by management for its own aims. This was seen in the example in the utility where the president of one consultant firm was drawn into a political intrigue, and the knowledge of behavior learned from him was used to help in a personal power fight.

Some of the social science theories that have been adopted by consultants are those of Maslow, Herzberg, **Fiedler**, and **McClelland**. Maslow proposed a *need hierarchy* that all individuals strive to satisfy. Herzberg applied this idea to the work setting and distinguished two factors of job satisfaction. One involves basic needs that prevent dissatisfaction (*hygiene factors*), while real *motivation* and satisfaction can only be derived from higher-order needs such as factors intrinsic to the job (responsibility and challenge).

Fiedler stressed the interaction of personality and situational variables—task structure, position power, and leader-member relations. He maintained that it may not be possible to teach someone to use a leadership style contrary to his personality and that companies might be better off placing a leader in a situation appropriate to his particular style.

McClelland spoke of the need for achievement, power, and affiliation as important motivators. His theories have been used by management consultants in motivation courses and organizational climate surveys, which can indicate which areas are problems in terms of workers' perceptions related to productivity.

When the activities of the consultants in the case study are examined, most of the social science theories are manifestly adopted, but latent functions expressed in political behavior do not contribute to the achievement of manifest goals. No real effort was made to provide for the workers' need for independence or autonomy, as Argyris suggests. Little was done to provide for meaningful participation, and while the need for less autocratic leadership was a manifest goal, it was not implemented.

The case study presented an analysis of the use of management consultants in a utility. The organization had a large operation of over 22,000 employees, providing steam, gas, and electricity. The organization was besieged with many problems: financial troubles, demands from external agencies, public concern about the company's ability to provide services, and pressure from the PSC. In addition, the EEOC, which charged that the utility industry lagged behind other major employers in the hiring of minorities and women, exerted pressure for changes.

The utility had been troubled since the early 1960s when a blackout of the entire city in 1965 called attention to its problems. Amidst the charges of inefficiency, excessive personnel, and poor customer service, a new chairman was hired to try to improve the company's image and, with his military background, to promote efficiency in the company. But the problems continued to mount. The pressures of the oil crisis of 1973, the lack of generating capacity, and the reduction of growth from new business created huge financial problems. The lack of capital—due to poor credit—dealt the company a severe blow and led to the suspension of its dividend in 1974. The new chairman was successful, however, in convincing the state to purchase two nuclear plants and to approve new rates and procedures that helped improve the utility's finances.

The relationship between the company and the PSC was a very important one. Since the PSC was responsible for rates, service, and long-range planning for all utilities in the state, it had great influence over the company's management. It is possible that the company's problems and the way they handled them were the fault of the PSC as much as the company itself. Since long-range planning was under the PSC's mandate, it was their responsibility to make sure that the company planned its future with foresight. The PSC recognized the company's problems but failed to take action until a crisis developed. In 1969 they publicly predicted power shortages, yet they allowed the situation to continue. By setting accounting and financing procedures that were unfavorable to the company, the PSC added to its financial difficulties.

The question can be raised as to whether the company wished to change or whether it wished to give the impression of changing while maintaining the status quo. The consultants who worked in the company, in retrospect, had little impact, yet their presence gave at least a semblance of a commitment to change. This image was desirable for the company since they needed to satisfy the external sources of the public pressures and the PSC, who had jurisdiction over the rate increases.

The company typified the high-slack environment with routine and repetitive functions, although it was now facing new circumstances. The organization also represented an axiologically not-good organization in that it was not aware of the interrelatedness of its parts, it was ineffective at problem solving, and it had a crisis management approach—not learning from past mistakes and ignoring the future while responding only to immediate problems.

Structurally, the company represented the typical pyramid-shaped hierarchy. In 1969 its organizational structure changed by creating geographically decentralized departments while maintaining centralized control through the top levels of management. Another significant change affected the power vested in the chairman and the president. When these two offices were combined in 1969, the previous president retained the title, but he was a figurehead without decision-making authority. With operating vice-presidents reporting directly to the chairman, the president lost his previous power. In 1975 a new president was permitted to become the CEO, and the position regained control over line functions.

The company used the structure of the organization to help in internal political maneuvering. For example, the president who lost power in 1969 when his office was combined with the chairman's was "promoted" in 1973 (two years before he retired) to vice-chairman to make room for a new president. In another case a senior vice-president of operations was moved to a staff position on the same reporting level as an AVP. It appears to have been done to remove the senior vice-president either because he was incompetent or, more likely, because it was a way to provide an opportunity for a replacement to gain experience while under the guidance of the soon-to-retire executive. On another occasion when an executive who was responsible for a program was promoted, he took the function with him even though his new office did not have responsibility for that task. This is unusual in that it is usually the office that determines the tasks that the individual assumes rather than the individual. An example of the office determining the tasks occurred when the responsibility of the general auditor's office was expanded to include the task of examining the company's operations and recommending improvements. This task should have been assigned or undertaken before that time since it is a normal function of that office.

These maneuverings are also reminiscent of **Jackall's** description of the organization as a nonbureaucratic, feudal system. In this case it seems like the feudal lord is taking part of his fiefdom with him as he transfers to another department.

Although some organizational changes and changes in personnel occurred, the basic structure of the company remained the same. As **Weiss** pointed out, the coordinative relationships that make up the organization's structure are relatively stable and change only slowly. Even with the change in leadership provided in 1967 by the new chairman, the organization did not change appreciably in its goals and management practices.

While in its expansionist phase, during which time it merged with other small companies, the company grew to a huge size. The law of surface and mass, as described by **Drucker**, can be seen in operation with the mass that enlarged in anticipation of continued expansion. Because of the oil crisis and other problems discussed above, by 1974 the company prematurely reached the limits of its market growth. At that point there was no new business and little capital for new construction. This meant that the mass could no longer be supported by the surface. The situation was compounded by the development of a new product (nuclear power), which decreased the surface. The sale of generating plants to the state aggravated the problem further by shrinking the surfaces even more.

Drucker believes, as previously mentioned, that there are organizations that are too big to function. Some experts recognized that the company was too large. A consultant realized that the company was no longer growing and therefore needed a reduction in management staff. **George Cabot Lodge** attributed many of the company's problems to its size and recommended that it be split in two-giving up the power generation and construction functions. In some measure the company did move in that direction since it purchases more power from other sources and has given the state the responsibility of building new plants.

The company's history of mergers and its decentralized form make it more apparent that it constitutes a large business consisting of smaller businesses. There is a need, therefore, to develop different strategies for each of the smaller markets (geographic and gas, electric, steam) as well as an overall corporate strategy. It is in this area that the company was criticized because they planned poorly.

With the creation of decentralization, as **Greenwood** describes it, it was predictable that conflict would arise between line and staff authority. In this company the chairman minimized this conflict by promoting line managers to the top operating management positions.

Several consultants were employed by the company during the ten-year period (1967–77) that has been studied; the majority of them were brought in within a two-year period (1974 and 1975).

### Consultant OAS

Top management brought in consultant **OAS** to survey management on their opinions and attitudes after there were threats of a management union being formed. Five levels of management were surveyed for areas of dissatisfaction. Most supervisors found many aspects of the company satisfactory and were generally proud of their affiliation with the company. A small percentage found factors such as direction by too many bosses, lack of consultation on decisions in their areas, and lack of advanced information about organization changes to be less satisfactory. Middle management was favorable in general on company benefits and felt relatively free to express themselves on employment issues and policies. Their misgivings revolved around the quality of employees and company morale.

While the survey was conducted, ostensibly, to cover areas of dissatisfaction, the general findings seem to have been favorable to the company (as far as can be determined within the limitations of the information provided). If this were truly indicative of managers' attitudes, it is hard to understand why the report was not circulated within the company. Since top management had the opportunity to meet with the consultant prior to issuing the final report, it is possible that they were able to influence its wording. It is more likely, however, that the findings were so favorable because managers did not feel free to commit their dissatisfactions to paper. This finding was also seen on the job satisfaction study, which indicated that, overall, managers were relatively satisfied. This may have been more apparent than real because people were afraid to speak out within a climate that penalized negative comments. As mentioned previously, the fealty relationships in this strongly hierarchical organization held strict sanctions against public criticism. Criticism was viewed as disloyalty or "insubordination" and could eliminate any chance of promotion. Managers were therefore unwilling to go on record with negative comments, although they were willing to confide in the staff trainers informally.

The consultant's entry through top management appears to have limited its perspective and restricted its activities to the request of management to only conduct the survey, without looking for other aspects or interpretations of results. OAS's brief intervention (four days) did not permit extensive involvement in the company. The results of the survey were used by the company to show the public and the PSC that the company was concerned about the quality of management and that they were trying to improve. The managers themselves, however, did not place much credence in top management's sincerity because no action was taken on their complaints. It did serve its purpose in stopping the movement toward a management union.

One might also question the professionalism even in the preparation of OAS's report. The report contained a summary and frequency distribution of comments along with the weighted averages for the group. There was no interpretation of the weighted averages or other results. In addition, it is difficult to interpret the tables as OAS presented them. For instance, the weighted average is an unusual statistic to present to a lay audience such as the company's top management.

The consultant's responsibility in this situation is usually to make sure that the client not only receives the results in numbers but that he understands what the numbers mean. Often this necessitates follow-up meetings in which results are presented and explained. The fact that none of this was requested by the company or done by the consultant raises serious questions as to both of their intentions.

## Consultant FLO

**Consultant FLO** was brought in to develop criteria for personnel selection. The precipitating problem was attributed to the JOBS '70s program: long-term employees complained that minority and female employees hired under the program were unqualified for entry-level jobs. During the EEOC hearings in 1971, an AVP had committed the company to securing the services of a consultant to validate selection criteria and to the continued hiring of minorities and women to reach affirmative action goals. Previously, the entry-level jobs had been filled by unskilled, poorly educated applicants who had been referred by company employees. Now that the applicants were coming from external sources and included minorities, there were complaints that they were not qualified. The long-term employees who were complaining had themselves been trained on the job. While the consultant was hired to establish objective job selection criteria, at no time was the latent source of conflict and prejudice addressed. Management did not wish to antagonize their long-term employees, whom they needed to maintain their productivity. At the same time they wanted to avoid EEOC charges of discrimination against minorities and  women. Bringing in an outside consultant allowed them to maintain the goodwill of everyone involved and to avoid pressure from the EEOC for some period of time.

FLO was engaged by middle management with the approval of top management. FLO had served as an expert witness for the EEOC on the subject of selection criteria and was considered an expert in the field. While FLO was given the assignment of developing selection criteria, the latent issues surrounding the problem were not dealt with by the company. FLO's system of selecting employees appeared to be a good solution to management's dilemma because it set up objective criteria that satisfied the EEOC requirements and did not bring up the issue of prejudice.

In this way the consultant served as an adjudicator between those who complained about the minorities being unqualified and those who were brought in under the JOBS program complaining of discrimination.

## Consultant BCF

**BCF** was brought in at the direction of the PSC—even against the resistance of top management. BCF conducted a study of the company's management and operations, and their findings went directly to the PSC. Their report recognized the problems the company faced that were beyond their control and areas in which they had opportunities to improve. Some areas for improvement were the company's management style, the need for expanded management and supervisory development, and the need to reduce the management staff. Because the report was issued directly to the PSC, its findings carried additional force and significance. The company appeared to be eager to respond to BCF's recommendations, perhaps so that the PSC would favorably regard the company's rate increase requests. The effect of their report was far-reaching; virtually all consultants brought in after the report was made were in some way linked to the company's response to this report.

BCF's assignment was to conduct a diagnostic phase as a study of the company's management and operations. To determine the problem areas, BCF interviewed managers from all levels and divisions of the company.

The findings of the consultant, as reflected in the report, made reference to the problem of the company's management style and referred to criticism the company had received for having so many former military personnel entering the company at policy-making levels. BCF suggested that top management diversify its approach and recommended that the company modify its management style. BCF also stressed the importance of developing more management skills at the executive and supervisory levels because many managers with technical knowledge lacked management skills.  The lack of broad-based management experience was partly due to the fact that there were no layoffs when the company made mergers with smaller utilities during its expansion phase; the lowering of the mandatory retirement age accelerated the loss of the more experienced managers. The consultant also referred to excess personnel and recommended a reduction in staff.

For top management BCF served to give visible substance to management's professed concerns. The hiring of other consultants was justified by the BCF reference to the need to expand management development. In addition, BCF reinforced the need for some type of action, a fact that had already surfaced from the public complaints and the PSC and EEOC hearings.

The finding by BCF that there should be a reduction of manpower contributed to the action taken later by the AVP when he fired 211 managers. He felt justified by the BCF report. The firings were also undertaken to show the public that the company was trying to improve efficiency before the next rate increase request. While the consultant was hired to improve the organization, the consequence of its recommendation was to cause problems—not the least of which was an age discrimination charge brought by some of the terminated managers.

As noted above, in their analysis BCF pointed out prior criticism of the large number of company executives with military backgrounds. It is obvious that the compnay did not heed the recommendation to diversify their leadership because they continued to hire ex-military personnel into such policy-making positions as employment director, vice-president of personnel, EEO officer, and other positions in the Employee Relations Department.

Although BCF recommended the establishment of an internal consulting capability to help broaden management's perspective, the company claimed that this was impractical since they were too short of broad-based management experience. It is doubtful that the company wanted to have internal consultants because there were a capable group of social scientists with broad backgrounds available from the Employee Relations Department. These professionals were more than able to carry out internal consulting duties, and, indeed, some did so on a limited basis. The company's objections probably stemmed from their desire to avoid analysis with a critical eye, which they had been able to accomplish with external consultants. Internal consultants might already "know too much" about the company to be manipulated easily.

BCF's relationship to the company was an unusual one for a consultant. It was selected by an outside agency (the PSC) and reported directly to them for the stated purpose of maintaining the consultant's objectivity. This procedure eliminated the usual negotiating that usually occurs as a consultant presents its findings to the client in preliminary drafts and, perhaps, modifies some of the report at the client's suggestion. While some errors may have gone uncorrected because of this (as the company bitterly complained), it seems to have been successful in ensuring the integrity of the consultant's findings.

BCF's style was also conducive to gaining objective, informed results. Their approach was a combination of task and people orientation. BCF was able to convey their interest in gaining information and opinions of others while maintaining their outsider, objective stance. BCF refused to be drawn into company politics, although the consultant could not prevent their findings from being used for political gains.

Once the report was issued, top management tried to use it to achieve their own aims. They used the report to justify the hiring of other consultants to show the PSC that they were taking action on the BCF recommendations. To show that they were reducing the management ratio, they fired the 211 managers while at the same time trying to get rid of the AVP who was responsible for implementing the firings. To give the impression that they were doing something to change their management style, they hired consultant ABC to supposedly create changes in the leadership style of managers while, in reality, not permitting changes to take place.

### Consultant ABC

**ABC** was brought in as a response to BCF's recommendation for additional management training and a change in the company's management style. Autocratic leadership had been noted as a company problem. It was mentioned at training workshops and had been confirmed in the BCF report. A consequence of the autocratic style was that managers became incapable of independent action because of their exclusion from decision making. The company indicated that it now wished to establish a change in style that would more readily accommodate change. The company also felt that the problem of its style would be increased with the entry of minorities and women who would tend to resist the autocratic methods.

ABC's assignment was to implement an ABC management training workshop on management styles. The consultant set about the task by training and certifying trainers within the company to conduct their program. The workshop also stressed communications, motivation, and conflict resolution.

Participation in the workshops was supposed to be restricted to the top 5 percent of management, while in reality those sent to the program were not necessarily the best performers. The elimination of older employees from the list of the top 5 percent ran counter to the espoused principles of the new, more democratic style. Failure to participate in instructor training was subject to threats and punitive action, which was in contradiction to the supposed aim of ABC's teachings.

In addition, ABC's knowledge of behavior was eventually turned into destructive infighting by company employees. On the basis of their new understanding of secondary needs and the behavioral grid, they were able to predict the behavior of one of the AVPs and to set him up to resign by putting him in charge of the reduction of excess management staff. The firing of the managers was done in such a way that it created a backlash: the age discrimination suit was filed and the AVP was convinced to resign. In this way the advice and knowledge of the consultant about behavior were utilized by the company in internal political warfare.

ABC appeared to be unaware of the abuses that emerged in the implementation of their program and ways in which their theories were being used for purposes directly opposed to ABC's teachings. ABC's main concern seemed to be in maintaining the personal relationships they had developed. It was here that they committed one of Reddin's errors—that of becoming emotionally involved with clients and being too concerned with being liked. ABC's style and approach of extreme people orientation limited their effectiveness. A personal relationship with one of the trainers restricted the information that was obtained.

When ABC was first brought into the company, there was some resistance on the part of trainers to an outside consultant. ABC was able to overcome this resistance by appealing to the staff as professional colleagues. The consultant offered the licensing of the trainers as an enhancement to the trainers' credentials as professionals. This inducement was sufficient to permit the trainers to put aside their critical thinking and to embrace the ABC program without reservations.

### Consultant CRY

The fifth consultant to be discussed in the case study was **CRY**. This consultant did not start out with the image of objectivity since the firm had a member on staff who was a relative of a client director.

The presenting problem was that there were no formal systems for reporting or scheduling work. The consultant's assignment was to establish a scheduling system for the construction department. The consultant used the task approach and was not at all concerned with developing personal relationships. The result was a system for monitoring the time and progress of projects and employees. The system called for forms that were not readily understood. More important, the system and the way in which it was developed led to increased feelings of insecurity in a department that was already under stress. Because of this low morale, another consultant (**BPA**) had to be hired to remedy the morale problem and to implement the CRY system. This is an example of the consultant firm believing that their responsibility ends with the design of the system and the client's not insisting that the implementation be included by contract in the assignment.

CRY did not recognize the human dimensions implicit in any change. What was seen as a lack of management planning created what Reddin refers to as "change overload" and left in its wake disappointed and angry employees.

### DISCUSSION AND INFERENCES

The final section covers the major theories referred to in this study and the implications of these theories on the consultants in the case study.

**Merton** spoke of latent functions as the unintended or unrecognized consequences that are observable and objective rather than subjective aims, motives, or purposes. This study of latent functions indicates that manifest intentions may be hidden to the company or the consultant or both or may be recognized but unacknowledged. They can be determined in some instances only after a study of intentions and consequences is completed—and usually after the stated (manifest) intentions fail conspicuously. Then the question may be asked, Why did we fail? Research at that time may indicate that in the original situation other, hidden intentions were present. These operate in addition to the conflicting intentions and actions; the lack of knowledge, and social, economic, and political realities that result in the fact that when dealing with human behavior in complex organizations, there are always unexpected events.

Consultant services are measured in terms of their contribution to meeting the goals of the organization; yet unintended consequences may occur that may be dysfunctional in relation to the stated or manifest organizational goals. It is important, then, to look for the latent problems as well as the presenting problems, and the latent outcome and unintended consequences in addition to the manifest results.

Table 5-1 summarizes the presenting problems; the latent problems; the entry, style, and approach of each consultant; and the manifest and latent outcomes of consultancy.

**Baritz's** observations on the co-optation and misuses of social scientists have been especially relevant to this study of management consultants. Management, in this organization, appears to have employed the consultants for a number of purposes; to enhance the company image, to pacify internal dissent, to conform to social norms, to enhance its power, to mollify external agencies such as the PSC and the EEOC, to delay action, and to justify rate increases.

Within this case study we have seen the consultant being employed to present an impression or an illusion, in the way that **Schein** describes deceptive behavior. Political aims designed to increase the influence of particular executives or to give the illusion of change when none was made were seen frequently in the use of consultants or the knowledge acquired from them.

Baritz regarded the social scientists as having compromised their professional standards by allowing management to use them in such a fashion. Little effort seems to be directed toward using social science knowledge for the betterment of the workers, although management claims to be trying to do so.

Some of the ways in which the consultant or social scientist may be co-opted were illustrated in the case study. OAS was used to enhance the company's image and to give managers the impression that top management was interested in their attitudes. FLO was brought in to pacify supervisors and employees who complained about the quality of new employees and to indicate compliance with the external norms created by affirmative action. Consultant BCF was hired at the direction of external forces, specifically the PSC. This firm was used to help enhance the company image for the public and private investors since it had an international reputation for improving management. External norms required greater efficiency and better use of personnel. The findings, however, were used by company officials for personal and political reasons. ABC was also hired to mollify external agency requirements for change. Its program was undertaken to reduce internal friction from complaints about autocratic and military management style. The knowledge learned about behavior was used by top management to increase their political control and to present the image that they were changing the company's management style, while at the same time they were using autocratic methods against dissenters. Finally, consultant CRY was hired to show the PSC that the company was responding to the BCF recommendation and to show the public that the company was becoming more efficient.

In conclusion, it is clear that (1) the rapid rate of change that is occurring in both the technical and management aspects of the organization and (2) the changes in the environment affecting the organization ensure the continued need for management consultants. Consultants bring their specialized knowledge, techniques, information, and training to a company, which has been gained from their industrywide experience. They are also supposed to bring, at least initially, an objectivity, critical analytical thinking, and the semblance of neutrality to company issues.

Since the presenting problem and consulting assignment form the basis of the consultant's work in the organization, their definition is extremely important. The examination of five management consultants who were engaged by a utility has shown that the executives of the company, who defined the problem

## TABLE 5-1
### SUMMARY OF FIVE CONSULTANTS IN THE CLIENT COMPANY

| Consultant | Presenting Problem | Unstated Problem | Entry | Style | Manifest Outcome | Latent Outcome |
|---|---|---|---|---|---|---|
| OAS | Survey opinions of management —find areas of dissatisfaction | Action by company in response to complaints of inefficiency in management | Top management | Unknown —brief intervention | Report on survey —responses submitted to top management | No action taken on complaints |
| FLO | Validate selection criteria for new employees | Pressure from managers that JOBS employees were unqualified, pressure from EEOC to hire minorities | Middle management | Task and people | Administrative manual for use of trait system of selection | Satisfied EEOC requirements  Satisfied demands of internal managers about new employees |
| BCF | Conduct a study of company management and operations | PSC directive that consultant be hired to restore public confidence  Justification of rate increases | PSC through top management | Task and people | Report issued to PSC and top management | Report used to justify firing 211 managers and ridding company of executive for political reasons  Report used to justify hiring more consultants  Age discrimination suit filed |

150

| | | | | | |
|---|---|---|---|---|---|
| ABC | Implement leadership training<br><br>Train company trainers | Pressure from PSC to implement BCF recommendation for new management style | Middle management via personal relationship | People | Workshops and instructor training | Identification of top 5 percent and bottom 5 percent in management<br><br>Received opportunity for complying with BCF recommendation for more management development<br><br>No change made in management style<br><br>EEO suit filed |
| CRY | Introduce scheduling and reporting system | Pressure to implement BCF recommendation to develop system | Middle management with sanction of top | Task | Planning and development of a scheduling system | Overload apparent in implementation<br><br>Hostility and low morale obvious in department<br><br>Necessary to call another consultant to implement system |

*SOURCE:* Compiled by the author.

and the assignment, did not articulate the latent, underlying problems to the consultant. In some cases they may not have been apparent to the company; in other cases they may have been disguised from the consultant for political reasons—that is, they served the function of personal power acquisition or work-related power acquisition and were purposely kept covert.

In this case study the consultants employed by the client had as their strategy the acceptance of the presenting problem as given by management and they confined themselves to it. This was illustrated by both OAS and CRY who did only as much, or as little, as management requested. Once the assignment had been accepted, it seems that the consultants were not able to ascertain information beyond the assignment because they limited their exposure within the organization by their entry through one part of the company, by their desire to avoid conflict between factions within the company, and by their desire to continue their relationship with the company in the future. Above all, it seems that the consultants did not perceive or anticipate under-lying, latent problems or consequences of their actions and as-sessments.

All of the consultants were able to produce from their own perspective a positive manifest outcome; that is, they completed their assignment. Few, however, were aware of the unantici-pated consequences of their consultancy. The client company itself was often not aware of the effects that came about uninten-tionally as a result of the consultant's presence.

These examples of co-optation seem to be inadvertent rather than deliberate on the part of the consultant and, at times, on the part of the company. Many of the consultants seem to have com-mitted the error of creating change overload, that is, introducing more change than the organization was willing or able to handle. Reddin emphasized that a rigid system, such as this company, can undermine any changes that are introduced. Brief interventions such as the OAS survey are particularly likely to have little direct impact.

The evidence from this company's use of consultants substan-tiated Ganesh's observation that entry through top management is necessary to ensure the possibility of making organization-wide changes. When personnel and training consultants enter through middle management, they have little likelihood of succeeding. The wrong type of entry can also lead to what Reddin calls "inappropriate attachment"—being confined to one part of the organization rather than forming connections throughout. This was exemplified by CRY because by entering through top management this consultant failed to get information from other levels; ABC, who entered through a personal relationship with an employee, was in a similar situation.

Since the way that the consultant goes about doing the assignment is an important factor in determining the outcome, the consultant's style and approach should be a consideration when selecting a consultant for particular problems in a company. The consultants in the case study used a variety of approaches, from the most people-oriented approach to the extreme task-oriented. In some cases, such as CRY, the style of the consultant actually created a climate of hostility toward consultants in general and toward the CRY system in particular. It seems that approaches that combine the elements of both people and task orientation may be the most effective.

As a result of the work of the five consultants who have been described in the case study, it can be seen that:

1. The final recommendations or actions of the consultant had far-reaching effects that were not necessarily those intended by either the consultant or the company; in some cases the findings or programs of the consultant were used in ways that were totally contradictory to the social science theories espoused (for example, ABC's participative leadership program); and
2. The presentation of findings coincided with the stated manifest problem that was given to the consultant; yet they still created a new series of problems and aggravated some existing ones.

The organization as a high-slack environment contributed to the misuse of the consultants' knowledge and findings in that there was ample time for political behavior within the organization and additional opportunity for the consultant to be drawn into factional intrigue. Overall, the consultants had little or no impact on changing the organization.

In the future it would be interesting to study other organizations to determine if these trends in the relationship between management consultants and clients prevail in other companies.

# Bibliography

## PRIMARY SOURCES

### Reports

Company Affirmative Action Reports, 1973–75.
Company Reports, 1974–77.
Consultant Firm Reports, 1971–77.

### Government Publications

U.S., Equal Employment Opportunity Commission.
*Hearings before the United States Equal Employment Opportunity Commission on Utilization of Minority and Women Workers in the Public Utilities Industry.* Washington, D.C.: Equal Employment Opportunity Commission, November 15, 1971.

### Periodicals

*Economist*, April 27, 1974, p. 251.
New York *Times*, February 16, 1951 through May 10, 1974.
*Wall Street Journal*, March 3, 1959 through September 12, 1974.

## SECONDARY SOURCES

### Books

U.S. EEOC, *Affirmative Action and Equal Employment: A Guidebook for Employers* (vol. 1). Washington, D.C.: Government Printing Office, 1974.
Argyris, Chris. "The Integration of the Individual and the Organization." In *Social Science Approaches to Business Behavior*, edited by George B. Strother, pp. 57–98. Homewood, Ill.: Dorsey Press, 1962.

_____. *Personality and Organizations: The Conflict between System and Individual*. New York: Harper & Row, 1957.

Atkinson, John W., and David Birch, eds. *Introduction to Motivation*. Princeton, N.J.: Van Nostrand, 1978.

Baritz, Loren. *The Servants of Power*. Middletown, Conn.: Wesleyan University Press, 1960.

Barnard, Chester I. The Functions of the Executive. Cambridge, Mass.: Harvard University Press, 1938.

Cartwright, Dorwin. "The Nature of Group Cohesiveness." In *Group Dynamics*, edited by Dorwin Cartwright and Alvin Zander, pp. 91–109. New York: Harper & Row, 1968.

Cyert, Richard M., and James G. March. *A Behavioral Theory of the Firm*. Englewood Cliffs, N.J.: Prentice-Hall, 1964.

Drucker, Peter. *Management: Tasks, Responsibilities, Practices*. New York: Harper & Row, 1974.

Dubin, Robert A. "Business Behavior Behaviorally Viewed." In *Social Science Approaches to Business Behavior*, edited by George B. Strother, pp. 11–55. Homewood, Ill.: Dorsey Press, 1962.

Dubrin, Andrew J. *Fundamentals of Organizational Behavior*. Elmsford, N.Y.: Pergamon Press, 1974.

Dun & Bradstreet. *A Guide to Management Services*. New York: Crowell, 1968.

Fiedler, Fred E. "Personality and Situational Determinants of Leader Behavior." In *Current Developments in the Study of Leadership*, edited by Edwin A. Fleishman and John G. Hunt, pp. 41–61. Carbondale, Ill.: Southern Illinois University Press, 1973.

_____. *A Theory of Leadership Effectiveness*. New York: McGraw-Hill, 1967.

Fleishman, Edwin A. "Twenty Years of Consideration and Structure." In *Current Developments in the Study of Leadership*, edited by Edwin A. Fleishman and John G. Hunt, pp. 1–40. Carbondale, Ill.: Southern Illinois University Press, 1973.

Freud, Sigmund. *Group Psychology and the Analysis of the Ego*, edited by John Strachey. New York: Norton, 1959.

Greenwood, William T., ed. *Management and Organizational Behavior Theories: An Interdisciplinary Approach*. Cincinnati, Ohio: South-Western, 1965.

Herzberg, Frederick. *The Motivation to Work*. 2d ed. New York: Wiley, 1959.

Hill, Walter A. "Leadership Style Flexibility, Satisfaction and Performance." In *Current Developments in the Study of Leadership*, edited by Edwin A. Fleishman and John G. Hunt, pp. 62–85. Carbondale, Ill.: Southern Illinois University Press, 1973.

Hodgetts, Richard M. *Management: Theory, Process and Practice*. Philadelphia: W. B. Saunders, 1979.

Janis, Irving. *Victims of Groupthink*. Boston: Houghton Mifflin, 1972.

Koontz, Harold, Cyril O'Donnell, and Heinz Weihrich. *Management*. 7th ed. New York: McGraw-Hill, 1980.

Kornhauser, William. *Scientists in Industry*. Berkeley: University of California Press, 1962.

Kubr, Martin, ed. *Management Consulting*. Geneva, Switzerland: International Labour Office, 1976.

McClelland, David C. *The Achieving Society*. Princeton, N.J.: Van Nostrand, 1961.

Mailick, Sidney, ed. *The Making of the Manager*. Garden City, N.Y.: Anchor Press, 1974.

Mann, Floyd C. "Studying and Creating Change: A Means to Understanding the Social Organization. In *Research in Industrial Human Relations*, edited by Conrad M. Arensberg, Solomon Barkin, W. Ellison Chalmers, Harold L. Wilensky, James C. Worthy, and Barbara L. Dennis, pp. 146–67. New York: Harper, 1957.

Maslow, Abraham H. *Motivation and Personality*. New York: Harper, 1954.

Mayo, Elton. *The Human Problems of an Industrial Civilization*. New York: Macmillan, 1933.

Merton, Robert K. *Social Theory and Social Structure*. New York: Free Press, 1968

*Moody's Public Utilities Manual*. New York: Moody's Investor Service, 1975, pp. 189–206.

*New York Red Book*. Albany, N.Y.: Williams Press, 1975.

Peres, Richard. *Dealing with Employment Discrimination*. New York: McGraw-Hill, 1974.

Radom, Matthew. *The Social Scientist in American Industry*. New Brunswick, N.J.: Rutgers University Press, 1970.

Scheidlinger, Saul. *Psychoanalysis and Group Behavior: A Study in Freudian Group Psychology*. New York: Norton, 1952.

Schein, Edgar H. *Organizational Psychology*. Englewood Cliffs, N.J.: Prentice-Hall, 1965.

Scott, William G. *Human Relations in Management*. Homewood, Ill.: Richard D. Irwin, 1962.

Stogdill, Ralph M. *Handbook of Leadership*. New York: Free Press, 1974.

Weinstein, Fred, and Gerald Platt. *Psychoanalytic Sociology*. Baltimore, Md.: Johns Hopkins University Press, 1973.

Zaleznik, Abraham, C. R. Christensen, and Fritz J. Roethlisberger. *The Motivation, Productivity and Satisfaction of Workers*. Boston: Harvard University Press, 1958.

## Journals

"The Benefits of Doing Your Own Consulting." *Business Week*, May 16, 1977, pp. 62–66.

Bowen, Don L., and Merrill J. Collett. "When and How to Use a Consultant." *Public Administration Review* 38 (September-October 1978): 476–81.

Brown, Rosemary. "Two Cheers for Consultancy." *Management Today*, April 1980, pp. 90–97.

Brown, Stephen W. "On Choosing a Management Consultant." *Arizona Business*, October 1975, pp. 9–14.

Canter, Ralph R. "A Human Relations Training Program." *Journal of Applied Psychology* 35 (1951): 38–45

Fiedler, Fred E. "Engineer the Job to Fit the Manager." *Harvard Business Review*, September-October 1965, pp. 115–22.

Fleishman, Edwin A. "Leadership Climate, Human Relations Training, and Supervisory Behavior." *Personnel Psychology* 6 (1953): 205–22.

Ganesh, S. R. "Organizational Consultants: A Comparison of Styles." *Human Relations* 31 (1978): 1–28.

Gouldner, Alvin W. "Cosmopolitans and Locals: Toward an Analysis of Latent Social Roles, I." *Administrative Science Quarterly*, December 1957, pp. 281–306.

Guzzardi, Walter, Jr. "Consultants: The Men Who Came to Dinner." *Fortune*, February 1965, pp. 138 ff.

Hall, Douglas T., and Khalil Nougaim. "An Examination of Maslow's Need Hierarchy in an Organizational Setting." *Organizational Behavior and Human Performance* 3 (February 1968): 12–35.

Holt, Herbert. "Applications of Psychoanalytic Group Techniques to Management Consultant Field." *Advanced Management Journal* 30 (January 1965): 37–43.

House, Robert J., and Lawrence A. Wigdor. "Herzberg's Dual-Factor Theory of Job Satisfaction: A Review of the Evidence and a Criticism." *Personnel Psychology* 20 (1967): 369–89.

Jackall, Robert. "Moral Mazes: Bureaucracy and Managerial Work." *Harvard Business Review*, in press.

Kaplan, Robert E. "Stages in Developing a Consulting Relation: A Case Study of a Long Beginning." *Journal of Applied Behavioral Science* 14 (January-March 1978): 43–60.

Kast, Fremont E. "Motivating the Organization Man." *Business Horizons*, Spring 1961, pp. 55–60.

Kelley, Robert E. "Should You Have an Internal Consultant?" *Harvard Business Review*, November-December 1979, pp. 110–20.

Kennedy, James H. "Management Consultants and Conflict of Interest." *Dun's Review*, March 1978, pp. 117–21.

Korman, Abraham K. "Consideration, Initiating Structure, and Organizational Criteria: A Review." *Personnel Psychology* 19 (1966): 349–62.

Likert, Rensis. "Measuring Organizational Performance." *Harvard Business Review*, March-April 1958, pp. 41–50.

Meyers, Lawrence C. "Some Effects of Facilitator Training on the Attitudes and Performance of People in Leadership Positions." *Dissertation Abstracts International* 31 (November 1970): 2962–63.

Michaelson, Lawrence K. "Leader Orientation, Leader Behavior, Group Effectiveness and Situational Favorability: An Empirical Extension of the Contingency Model." *Organizational Behavior and Human Performance* 9 (1973): 226–45.

Miner, John B. "The Management Consulting Firm as a Source of High Level Managerial Talent." *Academy of Management Journal* 16 (June 1973): 253–64.

Newport, M. Gene. "Middle Management Development in Industrial Organizations." *Dissertation Abstracts* 25 (1963): 164.

"The New Shape of Management Consulting." *Business Week*, May 21, 1979, pp. 98–104.

Radell, Nicholas J. "Optimizing the Management Consultant." *Data Management* 15 (August 1977): 32–36.

Raine, Ronald V. "Selecting the Consultant." *Personnel Administrator* 25 (December 1980): 41–43.

Reddin, William. "A Consultant Confesses." *Management Today*, January 1978, pp. 66–69.

Schein, Virginia. "Examining an Illusion: The Role of Deceptive Behaviors in Organizations." *Human Relations* 32 (1979): 287–95.

Shay, Philip W. "Toward a Unified Discipline of Management." *Conference Board Record* 13 (June 1976): 60–64.

"A State's Role in the Development of Power." *Public Utilities Fortnightly* 80 (August 1967): 53.

Tannenbaum, Robert, and Warren H. Schmidt. "How to Choose a Leadership Pattern." *Harvard Business Review*, May-June 1973, pp. 162–80.

Weiss, Robert S. "A Structure-Function Approach to Organization." *Journal of Social Issues* 12 (1956): 161–67.

## Papers

Dubin, Robert A. "Person and Organization." Paper presented at the 11th Annual Meeting—Industrial Research and the Discipline of Sociology—of the Industrial Relations Research Association, Madison, Wis., 160–63, 1959.

# Index

# About the Author

GERALD L. MOORE served on the faculty of New Jersey Institute of Technology in Newark as Assistant Professor of Organizational Behavior for three years before returning to private consulting in 1982. Prior to that, Dr. Moore worked as an industrial trainer and internal consultant for a utility and a financial giant from 1973–79.

Dr. Moore's business management and professional career began over two decades ago when he managed a multimillion dollar residential and business complex for one of the largest realty management consulting firms on the Eastern seaboard.

In the mid-sixties Dr. Moore joined the staff of the National Urban League as New York Area Project Director. A few years later he was appointed Executive Director of TEAM, a superagency established to help fight the war on poverty.

Dr. Moore opened his own management consulting firm in 1969 with a variety of organizations as clients from both the private and public sectors. He has consulted to several of the top Fortune 100 corporations, two of the largest medical centers in the East, and the largest legal corporation in the United States.

Dr. Moore has a Ph.D. in sociology, with a specialization in organizational behavior, from the Graduate School and University Center of the City University of New York.